SPECTRUM

Writing

Grade 3

School Specialty.
Publishing

Columbus, Ohio

Copyright © 2007 School Specialty Publishing. Published by Spectrum, an imprint of
School Specialty Publishing, a member of the School Specialty Family.

Send all inquiries to:
School Specialty Publishing
8720 Orion Place
Columbus, OH 43240-2111

ISBN 0-7696-8323-1

1 2 3 4 5 6 7 8 9 10 POH 11 10 09 08 07 06

Table of Contents Grade 3

Chapter 1 Focusing on Main Ideas

Chapter 2 Organizing Ideas

Chapter 3 Writing Your Own Thoughts

Chapter 4 Writing to Inform or Explain

Table of Contents, continued

Chapter 1

Lesson 1 See the Main Idea

Look at the picture. What do you see?

Playing games with your family is fun.

One picture can tell many things. If you look at the whole picture, though, it has one big, or main, idea. The sentence under the picture tells the main idea of the picture.

Now, look at this picture. Circle the sentence below that states the main idea of the picture.

Everyone loves the desert.

Animals and plants live in the desert.

Nothing is alive in the desert.

Lesson 1　See the Main Idea

Here is another picture. Write a sentence that states the main idea of the picture.

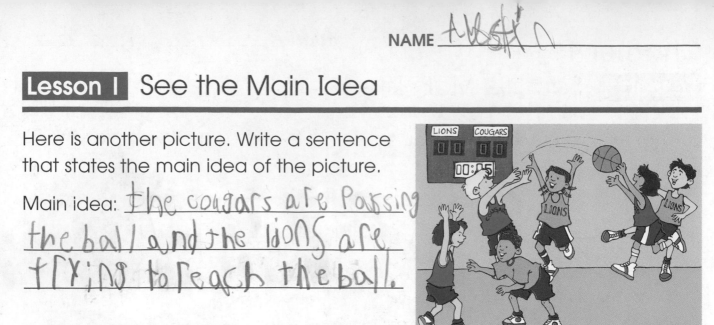

Main idea: ＿the cougars are passing the ball and the lions are trying to reach the ball.＿

Draw a picture in the space below. What is your picture about? Write the main idea of your picture on the line.

Main idea: ＿these people on theres balcony＿

On Your Own

Making a scrapbook is a fun activity. It is also a good way to save family pictures and memories. Get permission to use some family photos. Glue them on construction paper or a scrapbook page. For each photo, write a sentence that states the main idea.

Lesson 2 Add a Title

The title of a story tells what the story is about. What is each picture about? Circle the best title.

Keeping Busy

Out for a Walk

Alex's Bad Day

Building for Tomorrow

Time Goes By

City Plans New Park

Vacation Ideas

School Days Return

"Share Your Pet" Day

Lesson 2 Add a Title

Write a title for each picture.

Fetch

Vacatoin

9eting Food

Lesson 3 | Name a Story

The title of a story tells what the story is about. Read each story. Then, answer the question.

Molly has a problem. Her pet turtle will not stay in its box. Every day, it gets out. Mom does not like to find a turtle in the hallway or the bathroom. What can Molly do?

Molly goes for a walk in the back yard. She sees Andy playing in his kiddie pool in the next yard. Molly has an idea. She gets an okay from Mom, then starts to work. Molly puts some water in her old kiddie pool. Then, Mom helps her put some big rocks in the pool. Finally, Molly puts her turtle in. He looks right at home.

What is the best title for this story? Circle your choice.

Pets Are Hard Work   A New Home for Turtle   Molly and Mom

It was raining. Jake couldn't believe it. He had wanted to play outside all day today. He sat and watched the water drip down the window.

Jake got some crayons and started to draw a picture. He drew himself playing outside. He showed blue sky and a shining sun. Jake worked hard at his picture. When he finally looked up, he couldn't believe it. The view out the window looked just like his picture!

What is the best title for this story? Circle your choice.

A Weather Report   Jake's Very Bad Day   Rainy Day Drawing

Lesson 3 Write a Title

Read each story and write a title on the line. Remember that most words in a title begin with a capital letter. Only words such as *a, and,* and *the* are not capitalized. Also, the first and last word of a title are always capitalized.

Lokins Forward

Hanna had been looking forward to this day all week. It was "Dads and Daughters" day at school. She laughed as her dad tried to squeeze into her desk chair. Dad was glad when Hanna offered him a bigger chair.

After morning meeting, Hanna had a big surprise. The teacher called her up to the author's chair. She got settled, then she began reading a story. It was a special story that she had written about her dad. Hanna's dad smiled. He had been looking forward to this day all week, too.

Windy day

The wind tugged at Shawn's jacket and made his hair stand up straight. It was so windy that Shawn's buddies had given up on their baseball game. The pitchers couldn't get the ball anywhere near the batters. Now what could they do?

The guys were all sitting on the bleachers when a plastic bag went rolling along the ground. That gave Shawn an idea. He ran home for some grocery bags and string.

Back at the ball field, it didn't take long to tie a long string to the handles of a grocery bag. Shawn let go of the bag and up it went. It puffed up with air and bounced on the wind. Pretty soon there were a dozen fat white kites up in the air. Shawn thought it was a good ending to a sad baseball game.

Lesson 4 Find the Main Idea

The main idea of a paragraph is what the paragraph is all about.

Read the paragraph and decide what it is about. Then, circle your choice below.

Which game is older, basketball or football? Both of these games are more than 100 years old, but football, as we know it, got started about 15 years before basketball did. Soccer beats both of them, however. Soccer rules were first published in 1863, about 12 years before football's first game took place.

Football is older than basketball.

Soccer is the oldest game of all the sporting events.

The games we play have been around for many years.

Now, read this paragraph. What is its main idea? Circle your choice below.

I was up before 6 o'clock. I washed up and got dressed. Then, I set out breakfast for the whole family. By the time they got up, I had already eaten. I brushed my teeth and put my backpack on. Then, I sat on the front step. It was the first day of school, and the bus would not come for another hour.

I got ready for school early.

I made breakfast for my family.

I always brush my teeth after breakfast.

Lesson 4 Find the Main Idea

Read each paragraph. Then, answer the question.

> Snakes are interesting animals. They do not have any legs, so they move around by wiggling their entire body. They also do not have eyelids, so their eyes are always open. Most snakes can also swallow things that are bigger than its head. These features and more make snakes interesting animals.

What is the paragraph's main idea? Write it in a sentence.

_____

they dont Have legs ar eyelids.

> Getting lost in a crowd can be frightening. It is only natural for a child to want to look around for the person he or she was with. But wandering around is not safe. The child should stay in one place and wait. That way, the parents will be able to find the child. Parents should teach this as early as possible.

What is the paragraph's main idea? Write it in a sentence.

_____

it Could Be scary.

Lesson 5 Build Sentences and Paragraphs

You know all of these things about sentences.

- A sentence is a group of words that tells a complete thought.

- A sentence always begins with a capital letter.

- A sentence always ends with an end mark—either a period, a question mark, or an exclamation point.

When writers put sentences together in a group, it is called a paragraph. A **paragraph** tells about one topic. Read this paragraph about ferrets.

> I do not think ferrets are good pets. Ferrets cost more than other small pets, such as hamsters, gerbils, or even rabbits. They require quite a large cage, which is also costly. All small pets make messes, but ferrets are messier and smellier than most. Ferrets also chew on things and may cause harm both to themselves and to the things they chew on. For these reasons, ferrets do not make good pets.

Notice that all of the sentences are about the same subject: ferrets as pets. All of the sentences begin and end correctly. Also, notice that the first sentence is pushed in, or indented. Whenever you write a paragraph, you must indent the first sentence.

Read the paragraph, below. The paragraph contains two errors. Find and circle them.

> Hamsters are perfect pets. They do not cost very much, and they require a fairly small cage My mom likes the fact that they are quiet. I like the fact that I feed them once a day and clean their cage once a week. best of all, it is fun to watch hamsters play in their tunnels.

Lesson 5 Build Sentences and Paragraphs

What is your favorite kind of pet? It might be a
pet you have or a pet you would like to have.
Complete this sentence.

My favorite kind of pet is ___turtle___.

Write a paragraph about that kind of pet. When you finish writing, ask
yourself the questions at the bottom of the page. Make any corrections
that you need to.

_____

_____

_____

_____

_____

_____

_____

_____

_____

Questions to Ask About a Paragraph

Does each sentence begin with a capital letter?
Does each sentence end with an end mark?
Is the first sentence of the paragraph indented?
Does the paragraph tell about just one topic?

Lesson 5 Build Sentences and Paragraphs

Have you ever dreamed about having a wild kind of a pet? I mean a really crazy pet. It might be a dinosaur, a dragon, or a dog-headed lion! Write a paragraph about this kind of a pet. Tell why it would or would not be a good pet to have.

_____

_____

_____

_____

_____

_____

_____

_____

_____

_____

_____

_____

_____

Now that you are finished writing, look back at the Questions to Ask About a Paragraph on page 14 to check your paragraph.

Lesson 6 Stay on Topic

When you write a paragraph, write about just one thing at a time. If you stay on topic, your writing will be more clear and more interesting.

Paco wrote about planting a tree. Read Paco's paragraph.

> There is a new park at the end of the block. We planted an oak tree there last week. First, we had to dig a big hole. Mr. Orez put in some special soil. Then, it took three of us to move the tree into the hole. It was heavy! We all scooped the dirt back around the tree. Then, Mr. Orez taught us a goofy dance. When I was little, I took dancing lessons. He said it would pack the soil down so the tree could stand up. It must have worked. The tree looks great.

Paco did a good job with his paragraph. His ideas are clear, and he tells the steps of planting a tree in order. However, Paco put in a sentence that doesn't belong. The paragraph is about planting a tree. We don't need to know about Paco's dancing lessons. Paco's writing would be just fine without that sentence. Draw a line through that sentence. Then, read the paragraph again.

Here is what Mr. Orez wrote about planting the tree. Read his paragraph. Find and draw a line through the sentence that does not belong.

> The park is coming along well. The neighborhood kids had such a good time planting that oak tree last week. It took three of us to get that tree moved into the hole. Next week, I hope to have some flowers to plant. The kids looked pretty funny stomping that dirt down, but they were having fun. That is the whole point of this park.

Lesson 6 Stay on Topic

Paco's sister, Julia, wrote about the new park, too. Read her paragraph. Look for a sentence that is not on topic. When you find it, draw a line through it.

   Planting the tree last week was fun, but I can't wait for next week. Mr. Orez said he wants to plant some flowers. I hope the flowers have bright colors. I have a dress with lots of bright colors. They will look so pretty beside the playground.

Can you stay on topic? Write a paragraph about a tree, a park, or a playground. Make sure every sentence belongs.

_____

_____

_____

_____

_____

_____

_____

_____

_____

_____

_____

Chapter 2

Lesson 1 The Writing Process

Good writing starts with a plan. The best writers use the steps in the writing process to plan their writing. Following these five steps leads to good writing.

Step 1: Prewrite

Think of this step as the time to plan. Writers might choose a topic at this point. Or, they might list everything they know about a chosen topic. They might also write down what they need to learn about a topic. Writers might make lists that contain sentences, words, pictures, or charts to begin to put their ideas in order.

Step 2: Draft

Writers put their ideas on paper. This first draft contains sentences and paragraphs. Checking the prewriting notes will help keep the main ideas in order. There will be mistakes in this first draft, and that's okay.

Step 3: Revise

Writers change or fix their first draft. They might decide to move ideas around, put them in a different order, or to add information. They make sure they used clear words that really show readers what they mean. Writers might also take out words or sentences that do not belong.

Step 4: Proofread

Next, writers look over their work again to make sure everything is correct. They look especially for capital letters, end marks, and words that are not spelled correctly.

Step 5: Publish

Finally, writers write a final copy that has no mistakes. They are now ready to share their writing. They might choose to read their work out loud or to create a book. There are many ways for writers to publish their work.

Lesson 1 The Writing Process

What does the writing process look like? Melanie used the writing process to write a paragraph about her grandmother. The steps below are out of order. Label each step with a number and the name of the step.

Step _____ : _____

    Saturday afternoons are my favorite time. I go too my grandma's house then. We bake cookies. Usually, we bake our favorites. each week, we write a recipe on a card and put it in a box. Grandma is saving the recipes just for me.

Step _____ : _____

    Saturday afternoons are my favorite time. I go too my grandma's house then. We bake cookies. Usually, we bake our favorites. each week, we write a special recipe on a card and put it in a box. Grandma is saving the recipes just for me.

Step _____ : _____

cookies
special recipes
Saturday afternoons

Step _____ : _____

    Saturday afternoons are my favorite time. I go to my grandma's house then. We bake cookies. Usually, we bake our favorites. Each week, we write a special recipe on a card and put it in a box. Grandma is saving the recipes just for me.

Step _____ : _____

    Saturday afternoons are my favorite time. I go too my grandma's house then. We bake cookies. Usually, we bake our favorites. each week, we write a special recipe on a card and put it in a box. Grandma is saving the recipes just for me.

Lesson 2 List It

Making a list is one way to gather and record ideas before you begin to write. Trey is going to write about his favorite fruit. Here is his list.

grapefruit:
sour
sweet
sprinkled with sugar
pink
broiled
juicy

Mya wants to write about toads. She knows a few things, but she also needs to learn a few things. She listed what she knows. Then, she wrote some questions.

toads:
brown
lumpy
warts?
What do they eat? Flys
Where do they live? iN PoNds

Pretend that you are going to write about a food that you like to eat. List everything you know about the food. Remember to think about how it looks, sounds, smells, feels, and tastes.

Watermelon: They are sweet.
they Have seeds,   they are smooth and not
they are red and Green,   round
they are juicy.

Lesson 2 List It

Sometimes, writers use lists to help them choose a topic.

Imagine that your teacher has asked you to write about a memory from your childhood. You have so many memories, you can't decide which one to write about! Start by making a list of different memories you have.

_____   _____

_____   _____

_____   _____

_____   _____

Now, look at the list you just made. Think about each item. Is there one that is especially funny, or one that is especially important to you? Choose one and list details about it. Again, remember to think about how things looked, sounded, smelled, felt, or tasted.

Childhood memory: _____

_____   _____

_____   _____

_____   _____

_____   _____

_____   _____

_____   _____

Lesson 3 Sort Your List

Making a list can really help a writer collect ideas. Sometimes, making a list isn't enough, though. Sometimes, it is helpful to organize the items on a list so they make more sense. Look at Trey's list about grapefruit again. Some of Trey's words tell how the fruit looks and tastes. Some of Trey's words tell how he likes to eat it.

grapefruit: _____
sour _____
sweet _____
sprinkled with sugar _____
pink _____
broiled _____
juicy _____

grapefruit: _____

How it looks and tastes	How I eat it
sour	sprinkled with sugar
sweet	broiled
pink	
juicy	

Trey rewrote his list. He moved some items around and added some labels.

Now, look at Mya's list. She is still getting ready to write about toads. Could Mya's list be more helpful? Show how you would move items or add labels to make Mya's ideas more organized.

toads: _____ _____
brown _____ _____
lumpy _____ _____
warts? _____ _____
What do they eat? _____ _____
Where do they live? _____ _____

Lesson 3 Sort Your List

Look back at the list you made about a food on page 20. What kinds of words are on your list? Sort the items on your list so that the list is more organized. You might want to add labels, like Trey did, or just write the items in a different order.

_____   _____

_____   _____

_____   _____

_____   _____

Imagine that you must write about an animal for science class. Choose an animal. Then, list all of your ideas about that animal in the first column. After you make your list, look at it closely and see how you might sort the information. Write your organized list in the second column.

<u>List of ideas</u>   <u>My sorted list</u>

_____   _____

_____   _____

_____   _____

_____   _____

_____   _____

_____   _____

Lesson 4 Make an Idea Web

An idea web, or a cluster map, is another good way to collect and organize ideas before you start writing. Marco is going to write about his eighth birthday, which was a special day for him. He wrote his ideas and memories in an idea web.

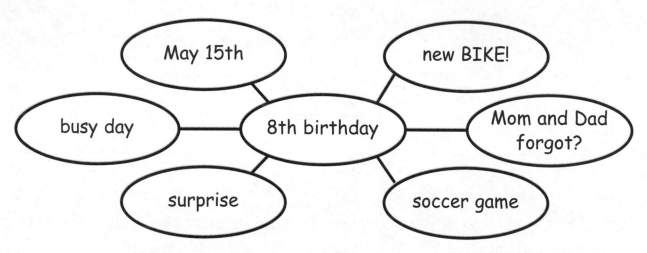

When Marco finished, he looked at his idea web. Some more ideas came to him, so he added them to his web. Notice that his new ideas are not connected to the oval in the center. They are connected to other ideas because they describe or explain the words in those ovals.

Lesson 4 Make an Idea Web

What special or important day do you remember? Maybe it was a birthday, the last day of school, or some other day. Choose a special day and create an idea web. If you need to, look back at Marco's web to see how he connected his ideas.

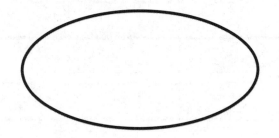

Lesson 5 Make a Time-Order Chart

When writers tell stories, they usually put the events in order. Before they write, writers might use a time-order, or sequence, chart to put their ideas in order.

Kay is writing a story. She made a time-order chart to keep the events in order. Here is part of Kay's chart.

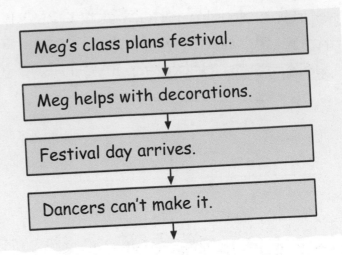

Think of a story about a festival or celebration. What interesting event might happen? Think of what events might lead up to the most interesting or exciting part. Record the events in order in the chart below.

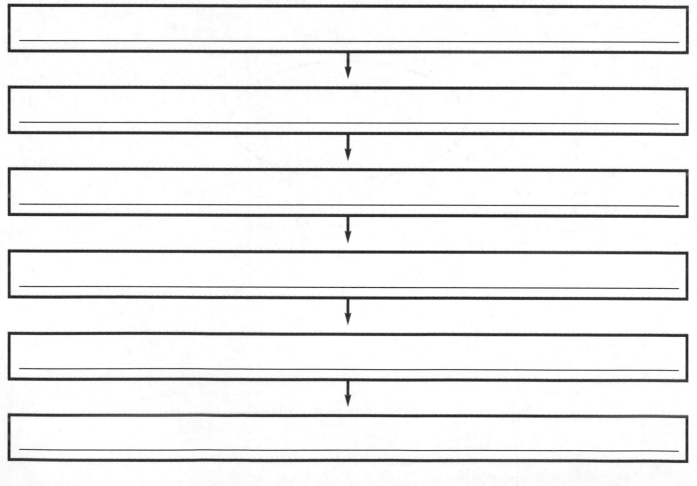

Lesson 5 Make a Time-Order Chart

Here is another time-order chart that uses boxes and arrows to show the order of events.

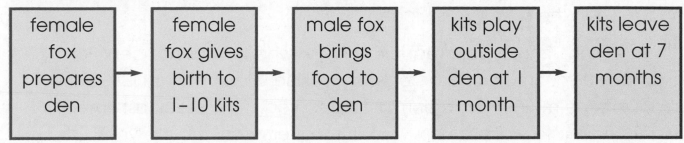

| female fox prepares den | → | female fox gives birth to 1–10 kits | → | male fox brings food to den | → | kits play outside den at 1 month | → | kits leave den at 7 months |

Think of a series of events that you know about. The events might be part of an animal's life cycle, like the fox example above. Or, they might be about an event that you saw or participated in. Think about in what order the events happen. Complete the time-order chart, using as many boxes as you need.

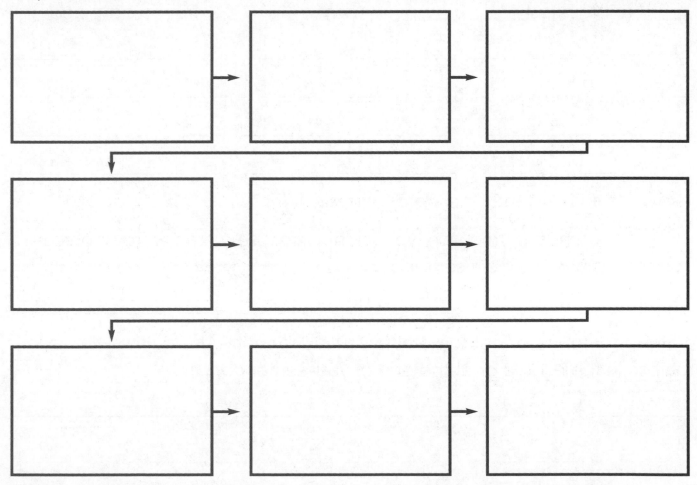

Lesson 6 When Did It Happen?

Remember those fairy tales that begin with "Once upon a time"? "Once upon a time" is not a specific time, but it does give some information about when the story takes place.

When writing, it helps your readers to know when things happen. For example, if your main character is just waking up, what time is it? If it is midnight, the main character might be scared. If it is breakfast time, it might be time to wake up anyway. If it is after noon, maybe your character slept through the whole day!

When could things happen in a story? Think of all the time words or phrases you can. Some ideas are listed below.

midnight   in the afternoon   April
at breakfast   today   three days ago

_____   _____   _____

_____   _____   _____

_____   _____   _____

_____   _____   _____

Now, use some of the time words you listed.

Write a sentence from a story you might write. Use a time word or phrase at the beginning of your sentence.

_____

Write a sentence about something you did recently. Use a time word or phrase in the middle or at the end of your sentence.

_____

Lesson 6 When Did It Happen?

In addition to time words, transition words help our readers know when things happen and in what order. Here are some common transition words.

after	as soon as	before	during
finally	first	later	meanwhile
next	soon	then	when

Here is an example of some transition words in action. Circle the transition words when you find them. Underline the time words.

Practice had been over for half an hour, and Mom still hadn't picked me up. I grumbled to myself. Then, as soon as she drove up, I figured it out. This was the day of her big meeting. She was all dressed up. That's why she had been late. Later, I said I was sorry for being mad at her.

Use some transition words in sentences. Use some time words from the list on page 28, as well.

Write about something that happens in the morning.

_____

_____

Write about two things that happen at the same time.

_____

_____

Write about three things that happen in order.

_____

_____

Lesson 7 Use Spatial Order

When writers tell about events, they use time order. When writers describe objects or places, they might use spatial order. In other words, they describe the order of where things are located in space. They might use a left-to-right or top-to-bottom order so that readers can get a clear picture of the object or place.

What is on the left in this picture? What is in the middle? What is on the right? Just as with time order, spatial order has a set of words that help us understand locations. Here are some common spatial words.

above	across	beside	between	beyond
into	left	middle	next to	over
right	through	under		

Look at your teacher's desk. Choose two objects. Where are they? Are they next to each other? Is one on top of the other? Are they close or far away? Write a sentence about the two objects. In the sentence, tell where they are.

_____

_____

Now, look around the room. Describe the general layout to someone who has never seen the room. Imagine that the person is standing in the doorway. Start by describing what he or she will see on the left, then straight ahead, then to the right.

_____

_____

_____

Lesson 7 Use Spatial Order

Would it make sense to describe a classroom from top to bottom?

> First, there is the ceiling. Then, there is the wall with the chalkboard. Finally, there is the floor.

That is kind of confusing. However, if you are in a big city, however, a top-to-bottom description might make sense as you look at tall buildings. A bottom-to-top description would work, too. Think of a building or structure you have seen. It might be a house, a statue, or a skyscraper. Close your eyes and try to remember just how it looked. Now, describe it from top to bottom or from bottom to top.

_____

_____

_____

_____

_____

_____

_____

_____

_____

_____

Lesson 7 Use Spatial Order

Steve needs some help. He is writing a story. His character is in a dungeon.
It is deep, dark, and creepy. The character is exploring the dungeon to see
just how deep, dark, and creepy it really is. Does the character start
describing things near the floor and go up? Or, does he look up and work
his way down? You decide. Describe the dungeon for Steve.

Lesson 8 How Important Is It?

When writing about an event, time order makes sense. If you are describing a place, spatial order makes sense. There is another method of organization that is useful if you are giving information or if you are writing to persuade. You can organize information by order of importance.

First, think about how a newspaper article gives information. Newspaper reporters know that their readers might not read the entire article, so they state the most important information first. In a newspaper article, the most important information has to do with who is involved, what it is, and where and when it is. Here is an example about a band meeting.

Band Meeting
The Drager Band Boosters will meet at 7 p.m. on Wednesday, August 1. All parents of band members are invited to attend. The fall schedule and new uniforms will be the main topics of discussion.

Write an article for one of these headlines. Make up details for the news story. Remember to give the most important information first. Tell who is involved, what the issue or event is, and where and when it takes place.

New Soccer Practice Schedule
Baby Panda Born at Zoo

New Rollercoaster Opens
Cougars Beat Warriors

_____

_____

_____

_____

_____

_____

_____

Lesson 8 How Important Is It?

When writing to persuade, the purpose is to make readers think or act in a certain way: for example, persuade classmates to vote for Jane Smith for class president; or, persuade the principal that an after-school nature club is a good idea.

When writing to persuade, save the most important ideas—the strongest arguments—for last. Build ideas from least important to the most important. Here is an example.

>   I think Jane Smith should be our class president. There are several good reasons to vote for her. First, she really wants the job. That means she will probably work hard. Second, she has good ideas that will make our classroom a better place. And, finally, she is a good friend to everyone and will work to build a strong classroom community.

Do you have an idea for an after-school club or group? Write a letter to your teacher or principal about the idea. Try to persuade the person that the club is a good idea. Save your strongest, or most important, reason for last.

_____

_____

_____

_____

_____

_____

_____

Lesson 9 Compare It With a Venn

To compare two items, a Venn diagram is a useful tool. Kevin can't decide whether to play soccer or football. He made a Venn diagram to compare the two sports. He wrote things that are the same about the two sports in the center. Things that are different about soccer are in the left circle, and things that are different about football are in the right circle.

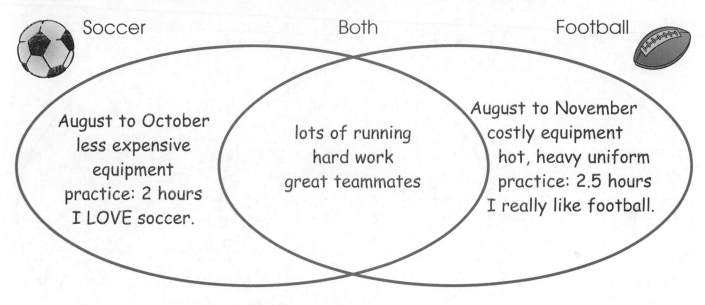

Soccer   Both   Football

August to October
less expensive
equipment
practice: 2 hours
I LOVE soccer.

lots of running
hard work
great teammates

August to November
costly equipment
hot, heavy uniform
practice: 2.5 hours
I really like football.

Now, compare bananas and lemons. Write what is different about bananas in the left circle. Write what is different about lemons in the right circle. Write what is the same about both fruits in the center.

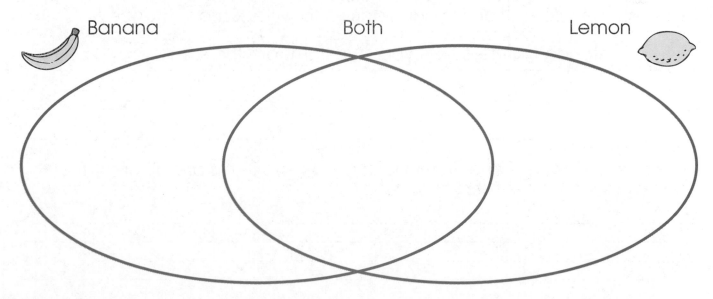

Banana   Both   Lemon

Lesson 9 Compare It With a Venn

What else would you like to compare? Maybe you want to compare third grade with second grade. Or, you could compare two books, two foods, or two kinds of shampoo. Choose the items you want to compare and label the circles. Then, write what is the same and different about the items.

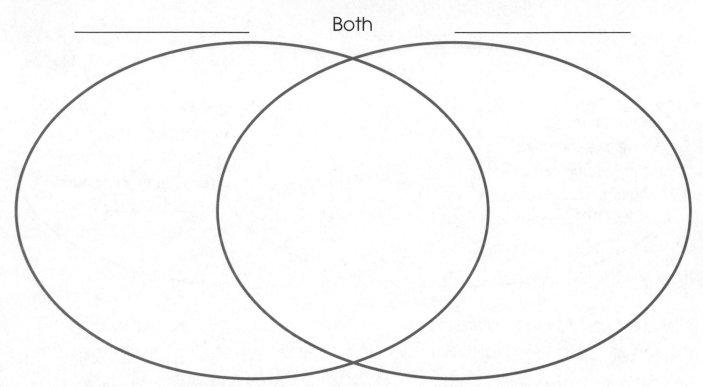

_____   Both   _____

Now, use the information in your diagram to write some sentences.

Write a sentence that tells how your two items are the same.

_____

_____

In a sentence, name one way in which your two items are different from each other.

_____

_____

Lesson 10 How to Compare

When comparing things, tell how they are alike and different. The word ending **–er** and the word *more* help describe how two things are different.

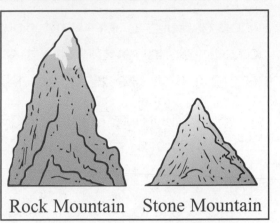

Rock Mountain is <u>taller</u> than Stone Mountain.

Notice how **er** was added to the end of the comparing word *tall*.

Rock Mountain Stone Mountain

Now compare the mountains using the comparing word *short*. Remember to add the ending. Complete this sentence.

Stone mountain is _____ than Rock Mountain.

Bo is *sadder* than Mo.   Mo is *happier* than Bo.

Notice the change in spelling of the comparing words *sad* and *happy* before adding the **-er** ending. For *sad*, add another **d**, then add **er**. For *happy*, change the **y** to **i**, then add **er**.

Now, try it below.

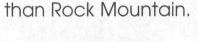

Sal is _____ Hal.

Hal is _____ Sal.

Sal   Hal

Lesson 10 How to Compare

When using a longer comparing word, do not add **er**. Instead, write the word *more* before the comparing word.

Dan   Stan

Stan's problem is *more dangerous* than Dan's problem.

What could be more comfortable than a bed made of boards? Draw a picture in the box. Then, write a sentence that compares the two beds. Use the word *more* in your sentence.

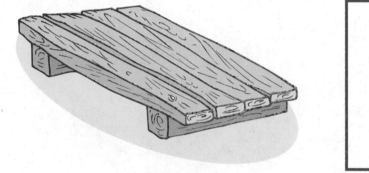

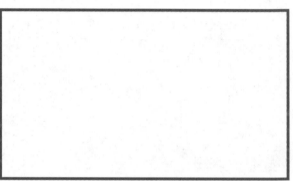

When writing about how three or more things are different, use the ending **-est** or the word *most*.

Ted is the *tallest* player.

What do you know about Tim? Complete the sentence. Use a word that ends in **est**.

Tim is the _____ player.

Tim   Tom   Ted

Lesson 10 How to Compare

Write a complete sentence to answer each question.

Which kite has the longest tail?

_____

_____

Which kite has the shortest tail?

_____

_____

Kite 1   Kite 2   Kite 3

Which kite do you think is the most beautiful?

_____

Compare the trees in this picture.

Write a sentence about one of them. Use *more* or a word with an **-er** ending in your sentence.

_____

_____

Compare the rabbits in this picture. Write a sentence about one of them. Use *most* or a word with an **-est** ending in your sentence.

_____

_____

Chapter 3

Lesson 1 Write for You

Many people write in diaries or journals. One writer might record thoughts and feelings that she does not reveal to other people. Another writer might simply record events and happenings.

Pretend that this is your journal page. Write about yesterday. It might have been a very ordinary day, but that's okay. Remember, when you write in a journal for school, someone will be reading it. When you write in a journal at home, only you will read it.

_____
_____
_____
_____
_____
_____
_____
_____
_____
_____
_____
_____
_____

Lesson 1 Write for You

Another way to record your thoughts and ideas is to keep a learning log. You might jot down a note about something you want to learn more about.

Lewis and Clark—What kinds of animals did they write about in their journals?

You might also record something you learn and want to remember. What have you learned this week? Write down something that you have learned this week.

_____

_____

_____

_____

In a reading log, you could keep track of everything you read. It becomes a handy list to remind you about books you've read, books you especially liked, and maybe even books you didn't care for.

What have you been reading lately? Record their titles and authors below. Rate each book, using words such as *excellent* or *okay*.

_____

_____

_____

_____

Lesson 2 Who Will Read It?

Dr. Platt is a scientist. He knows everything there is to know about platypuses. He is writing to a fellow scientist.

My study of *Ornithorhynchus anatinus* has taken a new turn. I am concentrating on the electroreceptors in their snouts. The species' ability to detect prey in this way is probably key to their survival.

Dr. Platt is also writing to his favorite niece. She likes platypuses, too, but she is only 8 years old. He tells her what he is learning about platypuses, but he uses different words than when he wrote to his scientist friend.

_____ A platypus's snout is very special. It has special nerves, or sensors, that can sense the muscle movements of its prey. So, a platypus doesn't even have to see what it's going to eat for lunch! It can sense a frog or an earthworm, even in the mud.

Dr. Platt wrote each letter to a different reader, or audience. He used certain words for one audience, and a different set of words for the other audience.

It is important for all writers to keep their audiences in mind. Writers must think about what the audience knows and what they don't know. They must also think about what the audience is or is not interested in.

Think of something you know a lot about.

What I know about: _____

What I know about it: _____

_____

_____

_____

Lesson 2 Who Will Read It?

Write a paragraph to someone who also knows quite a bit about your specialty. Share a new idea about the topic, or tell about something that happened. Remember, your audience also knows about the topic.

_____

_____

_____

_____

_____

_____

Now, write to someone who does not know much about this special interest of yours. It might be a grandparent, a younger cousin, or a family friend. What might you need to explain? What kinds of words might you need to use? Give the same information, or nearly the same information, as you did in the paragraph at the top of the page. Remember your audience.

_____

_____

_____

_____

_____

_____

Lesson 3 Parts of a Friendly Letter

A friendly letter is a letter written to a family member or friend. It could share family news, personal information, or some good news. Here is a friendly letter that Jennifer wrote to her grandmother.

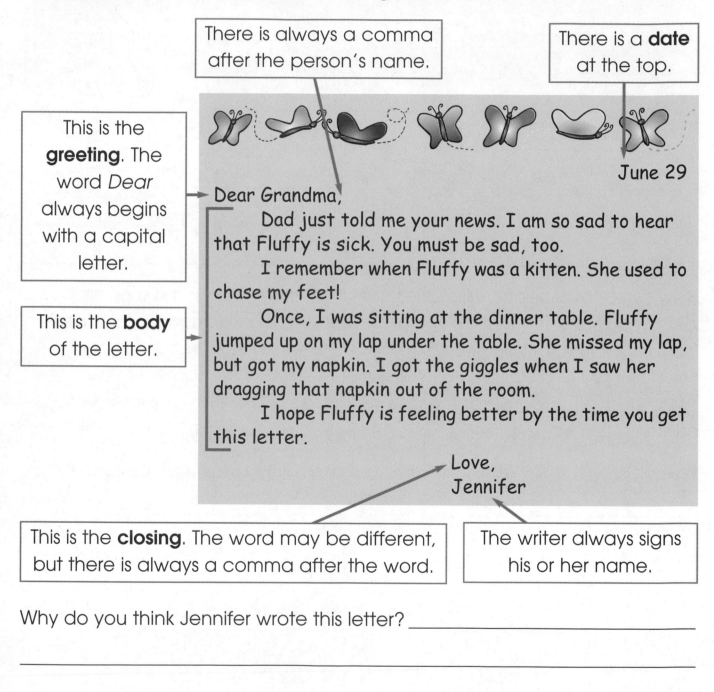

There is always a comma after the person's name.

There is a **date** at the top.

This is the **greeting**. The word *Dear* always begins with a capital letter.

This is the **body** of the letter.

June 29

Dear Grandma,

Dad just told me your news. I am so sad to hear that Fluffy is sick. You must be sad, too.

I remember when Fluffy was a kitten. She used to chase my feet!

Once, I was sitting at the dinner table. Fluffy jumped up on my lap under the table. She missed my lap, but got my napkin. I got the giggles when I saw her dragging that napkin out of the room.

I hope Fluffy is feeling better by the time you get this letter.

Love,
Jennifer

This is the **closing**. The word may be different, but there is always a comma after the word.

The writer always signs his or her name.

Why do you think Jennifer wrote this letter? _____

_____

_____

Lesson 3 Parts of a Friendly Letter

Grandma wrote back to Jennifer. Copy the parts of Grandma's letter into the right spots on the stationery.

| Dear Jennifer, | July 6 | Love,
Grandma |

Thank you for your letter, dear. Fluffy is much better, now.
I remember seeing Fluffy with that napkin. I went to the kitchen right after that. I had the giggles, too!

Lesson 4 Dear Friend

It is fun to write letters. It is also fun to get letters. If you send a letter to someone, maybe you will get one back! Write the name of each part of this friendly letter.

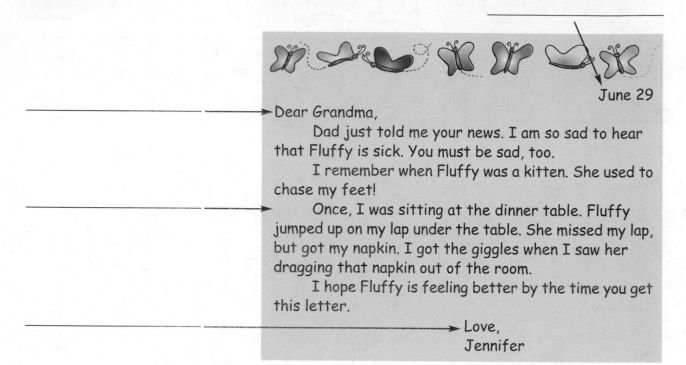

June 29

Dear Grandma,

Dad just told me your news. I am so sad to hear that Fluffy is sick. You must be sad, too.

I remember when Fluffy was a kitten. She used to chase my feet!

Once, I was sitting at the dinner table. Fluffy jumped up on my lap under the table. She missed my lap, but got my napkin. I got the giggles when I saw her dragging that napkin out of the room.

I hope Fluffy is feeling better by the time you get this letter.

Love,
Jennifer

Plan a letter to a friend or classmate. Think about what the person is interested in. What does he or she know about? Write some notes here to help plan what you might write about.

Now, write your letter on the next page. Remember to include all four parts of a friendly letter. Use your neatest printing or handwriting.

Lesson 4 Dear Friend

Lesson 5 Dear Teacher

Writing to a teacher is different from writing to someone who is your own age. You would not begin with "Dear Bart." You would begin with "Dear Mr. Maltin." What else might you need to think about?

Remember that your teacher is older than you are. He or she probably knows some things you don't know. At the same time, your teacher does not know everything about you, so maybe you can teach your teacher something.

Look again at the letter you wrote on page 47. Would that same letter be interesting to your teacher? Answer these questions as you begin to plan a letter to your teacher.

What general topic did you write about in the letter on page 47?

_____

Would your teacher be interested in that topic? Why or why not?

_____

_____

How could you change the topic for your teacher? Think about things you might leave out or things you might explain more fully.

_____

_____

What closing did you use in the letter on page 47? _____

Would you use a different closing for your teacher? If so, what closing?

_____

Write a letter to your teacher on the next page. Include all four parts of a friendly letter.

Lesson 5 Dear Teacher

Lesson 6   It Happened to Me

A **personal narrative** is a true story an author writes about his or her own experiences. Mick wrote a personal narrative about something that happened one day on the way to school.

> ### On the Way to School
>
> Every day was the same. I walked to school past buildings full of windows. I never knew what was behind the windows. Then, something changed.
>
> One day, I was counting sidewalk cracks, as usual, when I heard an amazing sound. Actually, it was lots of sounds. Someone was playing a harp. I looked around until I found the open window.
>
> I forgot all about school. I just stood and stared. I could see a lady with silver hair just inside the window. It looked as if she was hugging the harp. One arm on each side stroked the strings. Low notes and high notes came out all at once. I stood there until she turned and smiled at me. I felt pretty dumb for getting caught staring at her, but I smiled back. Then, she went back to playing. She didn't seem to mind that I was listening.
>
> Now, when I walk to school, I stop at crack number 144. I look up at the harp lady's window. If she is there, I listen for a while. We wave at each other. It's nice to have a friend to wave to on the way to school.

Here are the features of a personal narrative:

- It tells a story about something that happens in a writer's life.
- It is written in the first person, using words such as *I*, *me*, and *my*.
- It uses time and time-order words to tell events in a sequence.
- It expresses the writer's personal feelings.

Lesson 6 It Happened to Me

Why do people write personal narratives?

They might want to share their thoughts and feelings about something that happened to them. They might also want to entertain their readers. Often, people write to share their feelings and to entertain.

Who reads personal narratives?

If you write a personal narrative, teachers, parents, and classmates might read it. Ask yourself what you want your readers to get from your writing. What might they learn about you?

What can personal narratives be about?

They can be about anything that actually happens to the author. It might be a happy or sad event, a funny situation or a scary one.

What could you write a personal narrative about? Here are some idea starters.

my best day   my worst moment   my first swimming lesson
my greatest accomplishment   my biggest mistake
My picture was in the newspaper because….
how I met my best friend   I never worked so hard as when….
I was so embarrassed when….   I was so mad when….

Now, choose a few ideas that you like. Jot some notes about each one. One of these might be the start of a great personal narrative.

Starter: _____

_____

Starter: _____

_____

Starter: _____

_____

Lesson 7 The Writing Process: Personal Narrative

Writing a personal narrative gives you a chance to share an important or funny event with your readers. As you write, you may even discover something about yourself. First, review the steps of the writing process.

Prewrite: Choose a topic. Collect ideas. Make lists or charts. Organize ideas.

Draft: Write ideas down on paper in sentences.

Revise: Fix mistakes in draft. Add details. Change things around to make the writing better. Rewrite the sentences.

Proofread: Check for final mistakes in spelling, capitalization, and punctuation.

Publish: Make a final, error-free copy. Share with readers.

Prewrite

Personal narratives do not have to be about amazing races, life-and-death rescues, or unbelievable events. They can be about very ordinary things. Remember the narrative you read on page 50? Mick wrote about walking to school.

Look again at the ideas on page 51 and the notes you made. Choose one of those ideas, or another idea that you like, and begin to explore it here.

My idea: _____

List as many details as you can think of quickly. Remember the event and its sights, sounds, smells, and tastes.

_____   _____

_____   _____

_____

Lesson 7 The Writing Process: Personal Narrative

Choosing a topic is an important step. If your topic is too big, you'll be writing forever. If your topic is too small, you won't have enough to say. Here are some examples.

Shawna wanted to write about second grade, her favorite year so far. Well, a lot happened in second grade. That's too much to cover. So, Shawna tried to think about just one part of second grade. She wrote about her teacher, Mrs. Carlson.

Steve wanted to write about what he got for his birthday. He listed his presents. Well, there's more to a birthday than just presents. Steve's readers might be more interested in how Steve's family celebrates. Steve wrote about his birthday celebration and his presents.

Think about the idea you started to explore on page 52. Ask yourself these questions.

- Can I think of plenty of details to make my writing interesting?

- Do I think I can cover my idea in about one page?

- Will my topic be interesting to my readers?

If you don't think your topic will work, go back to page 52 and develop another one. If you do think your topic will work, begin organizing your ideas. Use the idea web below. Write your topic in the center. Add circles, as needed, to connect your ideas and details.

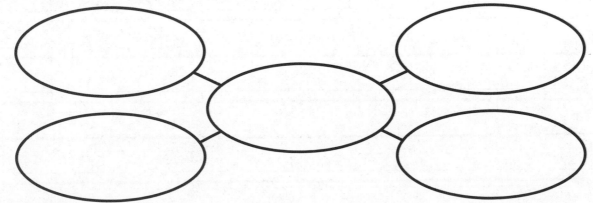

Lesson 7 The Writing Process: Personal Narrative

Now it is time to put your ideas in order. Think about the story you are about to tell in your personal narrative. Use the sequence chart on this page to list the events, in order.

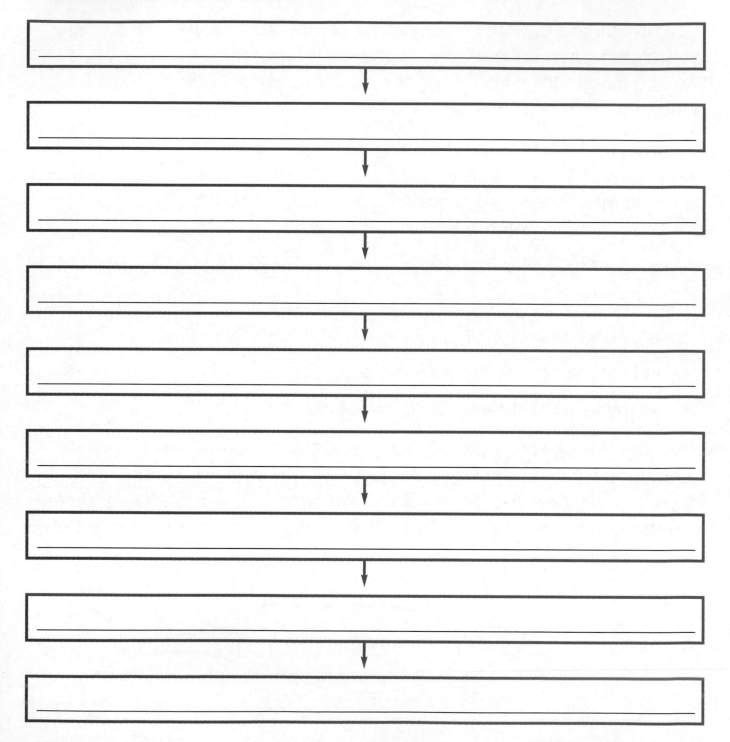

Lesson 7 The Writing Process: Personal Narrative

Draft

It is time to write a first draft of your personal narrative. Look back at your sequence chart whenever you need to. Write your personal narrative on this page. As you write, don't worry about misspelled words. Just get your ideas down in sentences and in order.

_____

_____

_____

_____

_____

_____

_____

_____

_____

_____

_____

_____

_____

_____

Write an idea for a title. It is okay if it changes later.

Title: _____

Lesson 7 The Writing Process: Personal Narrative

Revise

One of the hardest things for any writer to do is to fix, or change, his or her own work. Writers put thought and effort into their work. It's hard not to read even a first draft and think that it is perfect. However, good writers know that they can almost always improve their first drafts.

Answer these questions about your draft. If you answer "no" to any of these questions, then those are the areas that might need improvement. Feel free to make marks on your draft, so you know what needs more work.

- Did you tell about just one event or one "thing" in your narrative?

- Did you include details to make readers feel as if they are right there with you?

- Did you tell events in order? Did you use time-order words to show when events happened?

- Did you tell how you felt about the events? Do readers get a sense of your personal feelings?

- Did you use verbs and nouns that really say what you mean?

- How does your story sound when you read it aloud? Does it have both short and long sentences to make it interesting?

Look back through your draft and underline the action words. Did you use the same ones over and over? Did you use words that show the action? Here's an example.

The sound ~~happened~~ rang out again. Dad and I looked at each other. We ~~went~~ crept down the stairs. We didn't see anything unusual.

Lesson 7 The Writing Process: Personal Narrative

Write the revision of your first draft below. As you revise, remember to make sure your action words are really active.

_____

_____

_____

_____

_____

_____

_____

_____

_____

_____

_____

_____

_____

_____

Are you still happy with your title? If not, now is your chance to change it.

Title: _____

Lesson 7 The Writing Process: Personal Narrative

Proofread

Now is the time to correct those last little mistakes. Proofreading is easier if you look for just one kind of error at a time. So, read through once for capital letters. Read your narrative again for end punctuation. Then, read again for spelling. Here is a checklist to help you as you proofread your revised narrative.

> ____ Each sentence begins with a capital letter.
> ____ Each sentence ends with the correct punctuation (period, question mark, or exclamation point).
> ____ Each sentence states a complete thought.
> ____ All words are spelled correctly. (If you're not sure, check a dictionary.)

When proofreaders work, they use certain symbols. Using these symbols makes proofreading easier

> - T
>   three little lines under a letter mean that something should be capitalized. Write the capitalized letter above it.
>
> - If there is a period missing, do this⊙
>
> - Can you insert a question mark like this?
>
> - Don't forget your exclamation points!
>
>   this
> - Fix misspelled words like ~~tis.~~
>   ^

Use these symbols as you proofread your personal narrative. Remember to read your writing out loud. Sometimes it is easier to catch mistakes when reading out loud.

Lesson 7 The Writing Process: Personal Narrative

Publish

Write a final copy of your personal narrative. Write carefully and neatly so that there are no mistakes.

_____

_____

_____

_____

_____

_____

_____

_____

_____

_____

_____

_____

_____

_____

_____

_____

_____

_____

_____

Chapter 4

Lesson 1 Use Complete Sentences

You already know that a sentence is a group of words that states a complete thought. You also know that a sentence begins with a capital letter and ends with a period, a question mark, or an exclamation point. Here are some complete and correct sentences.

> Dogs howled.
>
> The wind blew all night.
>
> After the storm, we went out on the porch and looked at the fallen tree, which lay across the yard, covering the swing set, the garden shed, and the car in the driveway.

As you can see, complete sentences can be very short, very long, or in between. Here's a closer look at what makes a complete sentence.

Wind is the **subject**. It is the person or thing that **does the action**. *The wind* is the complete subject.	The wind (blew all night.)	*Blew* is the **predicate**. It is the **action**. *Blew all night* is the complete predicate.

If a sentence is missing either a subject or a predicate, it is not complete. It is called a **fragment**. Here are some sentence fragments.

> Walked through the puddles. (This fragment has no subject.)
>
> The water up to my ankles. (This fragment has no action word.)

Write whether each item is a sentence or a fragment. If it is a sentence, underline the complete subject and circle the complete predicate. Write *missing a subject* or *missing a predicate* next to each fragment.

The storm came suddenly. _____

Blew down many trees. _____

The wind so strong and steady. _____

Lesson 1 Use Complete Sentences

Sometimes, there is too much information in one sentence. When that happens, it might be a **run-on sentence**. A run-on sentence is actually two sentences that are joined without any punctuation. Here is an example.

The wind picked up I could hear it even in the basement.

To correct this, make two sentences out of the run-on sentence, like this:

The wind picked up. I could hear it even in the basement.

Or, join the two sentences with a comma and *or, but,* or *and.* In this case, *and* works best.

The wind picked up, and I could hear it even in the basement.

Remember, a run-on sentence is two or more complete sentences that are joined without any punctuation.

Write whether each item is a complete sentence or a run-on sentence.

_____ I heard a crash it was up in the kitchen.

_____ Mom went upstairs I stayed in the basement.

_____ She looked around because she was sure a window had broken.

_____ It was the cat he had knocked over a plant.

Look back at the items you marked as run-on sentences. Can you correct them? Use proofreading symbols from page 58 to show how you would correct the run-on sentences.

Lesson 2 Action!

Usually, the subject of a sentence does the action. That is easy to see in this sentence:

Zack blew a whistle.

The verb in the sentence is an **active verb** because the subject does the action.

What about this sentence?

A whistle was blown.

First, make sure it is a complete sentence. It has a subject and a predicate, so it is a sentence. *Whistle* is the subject of the sentence. However, the whistle does not do the action, the whistle "receives" the action. The verb, *was blown*, is a **passive verb**, because the subject does not do the action.

Passive verbs are always two-part verbs. They always have one of these helping verbs—*am, is, was, be, been*—plus a main verb. However, just because you see one of those helping verbs, it does not mean the verb is passive.

Passive verb: Anne **was** *pulled* in the wagon.

Active verb: Anne **was** *happy* to be riding.

How can you tell the difference? Ask yourself these two questions: What is the subject? Is the subject doing the action?

If the answer to the second question is "yes," then you have an active verb. If the answer is "no," you have a passive verb.

Sometimes, it is not known who did the action, so a passive verb must be used, such as, "The window was broken." Most of the time, however, writing will be more clear and easier to read with active verbs.

Lesson 2 Action!

Compare these two paragraphs. The one on the left is written mostly with passive verbs. The one on the right is written mostly with active verbs. What do you notice?

The parade was started right at 3 p.m. when a whistle was blown by Zack. The parade was led by Mr. Stoltzman. The first-graders were led in by Mrs. Kraft. Anne Connor, who has a broken leg, was pulled in a wagon by Amy Wheeler. The second-graders were allowed to ride their bikes by Mr. Garcia. The parade was enjoyed by everyone.	The parade started right at 3 p.m. when Zack blew a whistle. Mr. Stoltzman led the parade. Mrs. Kraft led the first-graders. Amy Wheeler pulled Anne Connor, who has a broken leg, in a wagon. Mr. Garcia allowed the second-graders to ride their bikes. Everyone enjoyed the parade.

Underline the subject of each sentence. Put an **X** next to each sentence that contains a passive verb.

_____ Tyler was watching the parade.

_____ Popcorn was eaten by everyone.

_____ Mrs. Kraft was surprised by the whistle.

_____ The mess was cleaned up after the parade.

Lesson 3 How To Do It

A process is a series of actions that lead toward a goal or product. You do processes every day. Getting up and going to school is a process. Eating your lunch is a process. Even picking teams for a game at recess is a process.

Mr. O'Malley says, "Homework is a process." Here are the three steps that Mr. O'Malley listed on the board:

1. Take the homework home.
2. Do the homework.
3. Return the completed homework to school.

The steps Mr. O'Malley listed tell about a simple process. Other processes have more steps and require a little more thought. They might also require instructions. When you follow instructions, you know that you must do them in order. When you write instructions, you must also do them in order, just like Mr. O'Malley did.

The first step in telling how to do a process is to list the steps in order. Think of something simple, such as making your bed or feeding a pet. What steps are there? In what order should they be done? Write them below.

How to _____

1. _____

2. _____

3. _____

4. _____

5. _____

Lesson 3 How To Do It

Remember your audience when writing. Who might read your instructions? Do they know a lot about the topic? Or, might some of the words or ideas be new to them? How much explaining must you do?

Imagine that you must tell a 5-year-old how to do something, such as play a simple game or put together a simple snack. List the steps here. Keep them clear and simple.

How to _____

1. _____

2. _____

3. _____

4. _____

5. _____

Read your two sets of instructions above and on Page 64 again. Is everything very clear? Did you use action words and describing words that say exactly what you mean? For example, if you told how to make a bed, did you say, "Pull the sheet up"? Would it be better to say, "Pull the sheet up tight"?

Find places where you might add details or change plain words to more clear words. Choose several steps that you can make better. Rewrite them here.

_____

_____

_____

_____

Lesson 4 Fact or Opinion

People like to share the facts they know whenever they get the chance. Others like to share their opinions, whether anyone asks for them or not. There is a right and a wrong time to use facts and opinions.

> **fact** *noun* something known to be true or real; something real; something that can be proven true
>
> **opinion** *noun* a belief; a personal judgment

When your teacher asks a question in class, he or she is usually looking for an answer that is a fact.

Question: What is the main ingredient in paper?
Answer: wood

That is a fact.

Think about this question.

Question: Is recycling paper a good thing?

This question is looking for an opinion. Here is how some students answered the question. They stated their opinions, and then they used facts to support their opinions.

Answer: Yes. Recycling paper saves trees.
Answer: Yes, because the landfills are filling up with paper.

Read these sentences. Label the opinions with an **O**. Label the facts with an **F**.

_____ Recycling paper is the only sensible thing to do.

_____ Recycled paper is less expensive to produce than new paper.

_____ I prefer recycled paper to new paper.

Lesson 4 Fact or Opinion

When writing, be careful when it comes to facts and opinions. Make sure you are writing facts. If you are writing opinions, make sure they were asked for. Also, make sure you support your opinions with facts.

Think of a subject about which you have an opinion. It might be recycling, school uniforms, or your favorite music. Write two opinions about the subject.

Opinion 1:_____

_____

Opinion 2:_____

_____

Now, write two facts about the same subject.

Fact 1: _____

_____

Fact 2: _____

_____

Finally, write an opinion and support it with a fact. If you need to, look back at page 66 to see how the students supported their opinions about recycling paper.

_____

_____

_____

_____

Lesson 5 This Is How It Happened

Paul saw a basketball game last night, and it was a great game. His school's team won, and he is eager to write about it for the school newspaper. His first step was to list the important events in order.

1. At half time, the Bobcats were behind by 12 points.
2. Teams returned to the floor, and the Bobcats were fired up.
3. The Bobcats scored 10 points before the Bulldogs even knew what happened.
4. The teams traded baskets right up to the final seconds.
5. Jackson made the play of the night, pushing the Bobcats ahead by 2 points to win.

Paul included important details from the game, and he put them in order. He also included some opinions. In item #2, "the Bobcats were fired up" is an opinion. Can you find two other opinions in the list? Circle them.

Paul's opinions make the information about the game more interesting. They help you feel as if you were there, watching the action.

Here is a list of events from the Bulldogs' point of view. Like Paul's list, it gives events in order. Also like Paul, the writer included opinions. When you find them, circle them.

1. The Bulldogs played very well during the first half.
2. At half time, they led the game by 12.
3. The Bulldogs started the second half with a little too much confidence.
4. The Bobcats went on a scoring streak.
5. The Bulldogs were unable to stop the Bobcats from making the winning basket.

Lesson 5 This Is How It Happened

Think about what you have done so far today. List some of today's events, in order. If you include any opinions, circle them.

1. _____

2. _____

3. _____

4. _____

5. _____

Now, think of something a little more exciting. Think of an event that you have seen or been to recently. It might be a sporting event, a concert, or a neighborhood party. Write some of the important or interesting things that happened in order. If you include opinions, circle them.

1. _____

_____

2. _____

_____

3. _____

_____

4. _____

_____

5. _____

_____

Lesson 6 Special Instructions

Have you ever looked at the instructions for putting together a bicycle? Did they look pretty tough? That's because those instructions were written for an adult. The writer assumed that an adult would know about certain tools and how to use them.

Write instructions for making a greeting card. Your instructions will be included in a book of project ideas for first-graders. You need to make your instructions simple and clear for your first-grade readers. Remember to put the steps in order. Include drawings in the space on the right if you think they will help your readers understand.

How to Make a Greeting Card
(for first-graders)

_____

_____

_____

_____

_____

_____

_____

_____

_____

Lesson 6 Special Instructions

Your greeting card ideas are so good that you have been asked to write some more instructions. This time, they will be for teenagers. How might you need to change your instructions for your teenage readers? What details might you add to make the project interesting to or challenging for teenagers? Write your new set of instructions here. Include drawings if you think they will be helpful. It is still important to put the steps in order.

How to Make a Greeting Card
(for teenagers)

_____

_____

_____

_____

_____

_____

_____

_____

_____

_____

_____

_____

Lesson 7 It Is Just Around the Corner

You are walking into the lunchroom when a new
student walks up and asks you how to get to the
nurse's office. Do you know the way? Can you give
clear directions to help the other student find the way?

Directions, just like how-to instructions, need to be in order. They also need
to tell *where*. Here are some words to help you write clear directions.

Direction Words	Position Words	Time-Order Words
left	over	first
right	under	second
up	past	then
down	beyond	next
north	before	after that
west	above	finally
	beside	

At Jamie's school, this is how to get from the lunchroom to the nurse's
office. Notice how Jamie uses some of the words from the lists above.
Circle each one that you find.

    First, go down this hallway. When you get to the end, turn left.
Walk past the main office. Then, the nurse's office is the second door on
the right.

Lesson 7 It Is Just Around the Corner

Write directions that tell how to get from your classroom to the lunchroom. If you need to, close your eyes and imagine yourself walking there. Now, write your directions. If you need to, look back on page 72 for direction, position, and time-order words to use.

_____

_____

_____

_____

_____

Imagine you live in a castle on a hill. You have to walk all the way to the next hill to get to school. Between your castle and the school is a town. What streets must you follow? How do you know where to turn? If it helps, draw a sketch that shows the castle,  the town, and the school. Write directions to help someone find the way.

_____

_____

_____

_____

_____

Lesson 8 Ask the Right Question

The first lesson that reporters learn is how to ask questions. And their questions are always based on the words *who, what, when, where, why,* and *how.* You can use these questions, too, to find out many things.

Beth's class is studying families. Beth is supposed to ask a family member some questions. She started planning her questions below. Can you finish Beth's questions for her? Think about the kinds of questions you would ask a family member.

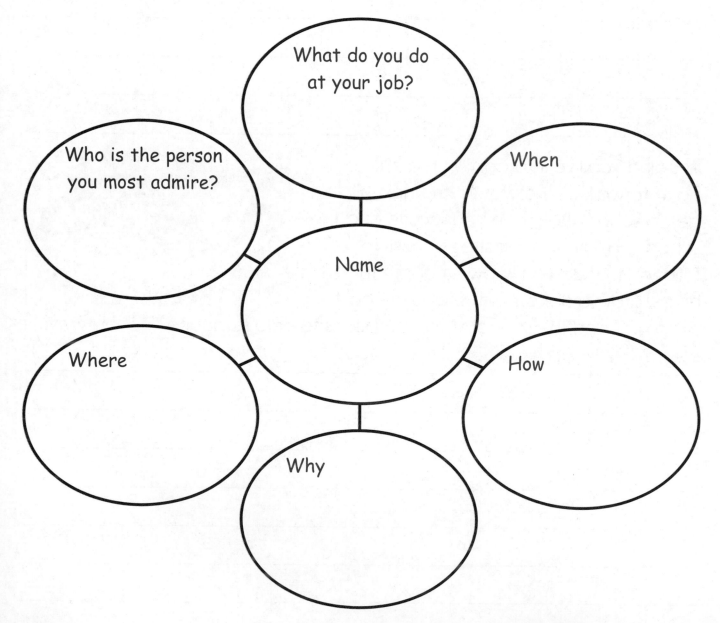

Lesson 8 Ask the Right Question

If you could interview anyone in the world, whom would you choose? Would it be the president or some other world leader? Would it be a doctor, a musician, or an astronaut? Remember, it could be anyone.

Imagine your interview is next week. Now, prepare your questions. What will you ask this special person? You may ask more than one question with each question word. Write your questions below.

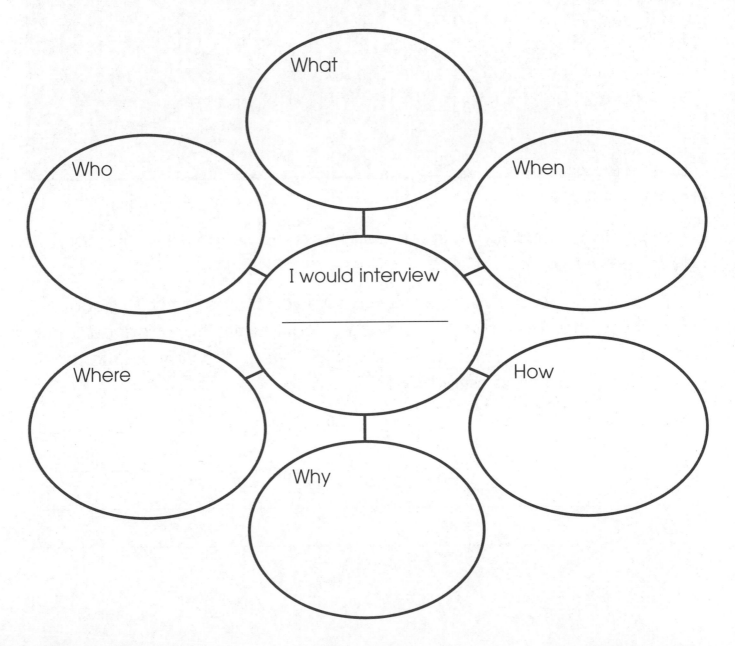

Lesson 9 The Writing Process: News Story

A news story is an account of something that has happened. A news story might be about a natural disaster, such as a storm or an earthquake. Or, it might be about the circus that came to town.

Before you write a news story, review the steps of the writing process.

Prewrite: Choose a topic. Collect ideas. Make lists or charts. Organize ideas.

Draft: Write ideas down on paper in sentences.

Revise: Fix mistakes in draft. Add details. Change things around to make the writing better. Rewrite the sentences.

Proofread: Check for final mistakes in spelling, capitalization, and punctuation.

Publish: Make a final, error-free copy. Share with readers.

Prewrite

Every city, town, and village in the world has news, even if it is important only to the people in that place.

What news story would you like to write? Will you choose to write about a famous person or a person you know? You could write about penguins in Antarctica, the fish in a local river, a new invention, or a very old machine. Write some possible topics for news stories here.

_____   _____

_____   _____

_____   _____

Lesson 9 The Writing Process: News Story

Look over the ideas you recorded on page 76. Which one seems the best? Choose one and write it below.

My idea: _____

What do you know about this topic? What might you need to learn about this topic? Write down pieces of information that you know or need to find out.

_____   _____

_____   _____

_____   _____

_____   _____

Even if you're not interviewing a person, you can still ask yourself questions that begin with *who, what, where, when, why,* and *how.* Asking these questions will provide information to you. Think of questions that you would like to answer in your news story. Write them here.

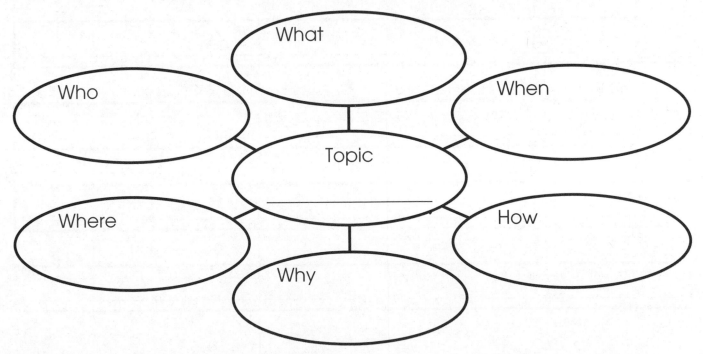

Lesson 9 The Writing Process: News Story

So far, you have been choosing a topic and collecting ideas. Now it is time to put your ideas in order. Think about the news story you are about to write. Use the sequence chart on this page to put your information into an order that makes sense. You might use time order, order of importance, or spatial order. Think about what fits best with your topic.

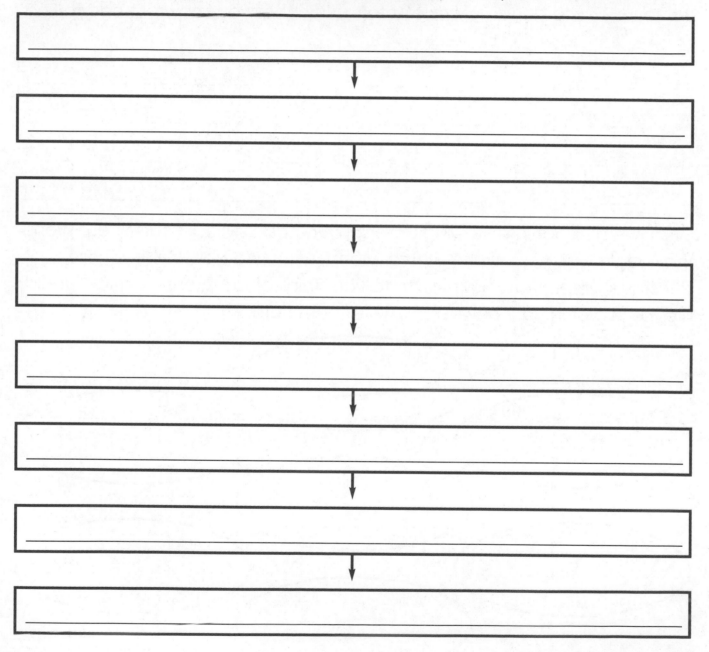

Lesson 9 The Writing Process: News Story

Draft

It is time to write a first draft of your news story. As you write, look at the chart on page 78 to keep your ideas in order. Write your news story on this page. Continue on another sheet of paper if you need to. Do not worry about misspelled words or punctuation for now. Just write your ideas down in sentences and in order.

_____

_____

_____

_____

_____

_____

_____

_____

_____

_____

_____

_____

Write an idea for a headline here. You can change it later.

Headline: 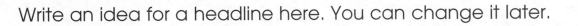 _____

Lesson 9 The Writing Process: News Story

Revise

People who write news stories know that they must look over their work carefully. Once it is printed in the newspaper, it is too late to fix a mistake. So, they reread their news stories and think about ways to make them better. Here are some questions to ask about the first draft of your own news story. If you answer "no" to any of these questions, those are the areas that might need improvement. Feel free to make marks on your draft, so you know what needs more work.

- Does your news story answer the questions *Who*?, *What*?, *Where*?, *When*?, *Why*?, and *How*?
- Is the information in your news story clearly presented? Do details fit together in a way that makes sense to readers?
- If you expressed opinions, did you support them with facts?
- Does your news story begin with a sentence that grabs readers' attention and makes them want to keep reading?
- Will readers get the idea that you are interested in this topic? Did you give them a sense of why the topic is interesting?
- Did you use verbs and nouns that really say what you mean?
- Did you read your news story out loud? Did you include sentences of different lengths to make it sound interesting?

First, focus on making sure your information is correct and that it will be clear to your readers. Look back through your draft and underline the facts. Are you sure about all of them? Do you need to check an encyclopedia or the person you interviewed again? Now is the time to make sure everything is correct.

Lesson 9 The Writing Process: News Story

Write the revision of your first draft here. As you revise, keep your audience in mind. Make sure you are presenting information in a clear manner.

_____

_____

_____

_____

_____

_____

_____

_____

_____

_____

_____

_____

_____

_____

Now that you have revised your draft, are you still happy with your headline? If not, write a new one below.

Headline: _____

Lesson 9 The Writing Process: News Story

Proofread

Now, correct the last mistakes. Proofreading is easier if you look for just one kind of error at a time. First, read through it once for capital letters. Read it again for end punctuation. Then, read it again for spelling. Here is a checklist to help you as you proofread your revised news story.

> _____ Each sentence begins with a capital letter.
> _____ Each sentence ends with the correct punctuation (period, question mark, or exclamation point).
> _____ Each sentence states a complete thought.
> _____ All words are spelled correctly.

When proofreaders work, they use certain symbols. Using these symbols makes their job easier. They will make your job easier, too.

> • three little lines under a letter mean that something should be capitalized. Write the capitalized letter above it.
>
> • If there is a period missing, do this⊙
>
> • Can you insert a question mark like this?
>
> • Don't forget your exclamation points!
>
> • Fix misspelled words like this.

Use these symbols as you proofread your news story. Remember to read your writing out loud, even if there is no one to listen. Sometimes it is easier to catch mistakes when reading out loud.

Lesson 9 The Writing Process: News Story

Publish

On page 83, write a final copy of your news story. When you are finished, share your news story with a friend or classmate.

_____

_____

_____

_____

_____

_____

_____

_____

_____

_____

_____

_____

_____

_____

Chapter 5
Lesson 1 Use Your Senses

If you were standing in this kitchen, just think what would be around you. You would see the steaming plates of food and hear the clattering of pans. You would surely smell a mixture of foods lined up on the smooth countertop. And, if you were lucky, you would get to taste something salty, spicy, or sweet. In other words, you would learn about the kitchen by using all five of your senses: seeing, hearing, smelling, touching, and tasting.

If you were to describe this kitchen to someone else, you should use all five of your senses. How do you use your senses when you write? You use words that help readers use their senses.

Look again at the picture. What do you see? List some things here. Remember to help your reader see things, too. For example, do you see a "large pot," or a "large, red pot"?

What I see: _____ _____

_____ _____ _____

Now, use your other senses and write what you would hear, smell, touch, and taste in this kitchen.

What I hear: _____ _____

What I smell: _____ _____

What I touch: _____ _____

What I taste: _____ _____

Lesson 1 | Use Your Senses

Look back at the lists you made on page 84. Did you remember to use good sense words so that readers can see, hear, smell, touch, and taste what is in the kitchen? For example, if you said that you hear voices in this kitchen, ask yourself what kind of voices they might be. Are they happy, angry, quiet, or loud ones? Review your list, and see if you can add any other words that more clearly describe the kitchen.

Now, put your words to work. Describe this kitchen so clearly that your reader will feel as if he or she is actually standing right in the middle of it. For this paragraph, organize your ideas by sense. First, tell what you saw, then what you heard, then what you smelled, touched, and tasted. Remember to indent the first sentence of your paragraph.

_____

_____

_____

_____

_____

_____

_____

_____

_____

_____

_____

Lesson 2 Make a Riddle

You can put your senses to work and make some riddles. Here is a riddle that Tam wrote.

> What is long and skinny, soft on one end and pointed at the other, and gets smaller as you use it?

Do you know what it is? You probably have one on your desk right now. It is a pencil.

For her riddle, Tam used a common object and turned it into a mystery. She told what it looks like, long and skinny, and how it feels, soft and pointed. Then, she added one other detail, gets smaller, to make her riddle interesting.

Write your own riddle. Use a sheet of paper as the answer of the riddle. First, use your senses to learn about the paper. Some details are already filled in for you.

What does a piece of paper

look like? _____

smell like? __has no smell_____

sound like? _____

feel like? _____

taste like? __(does not apply)_____

Now, use what you know about this piece of paper to write a riddle.

What is _____

_____

Lesson 2 Make a Riddle

Write another riddle, this time using a book as the answer. Record some details here. Then, write your riddle.

What does a book

look like? _____

smell like? _____

sound like? _____

feel like? _____

taste like? _____

Riddle: _____

_____

Choose another common object, but don't tell anyone what you're choosing. Record details about the object here. Then, write a riddle and share it with someone. See how long it takes your reader to guess the answer.

What does a _____

look like? _____

smell like? _____

sound like? _____

feel like? _____

taste like? _____

Riddle: _____

_____

Lesson 3 This Is A Room

If you walked into this room, you would probably look from one side to the other. Most likely, you would look to the left first, then the center, and then to the right. List some details about the room here.

On the left	In the center	On the right

Organizing details from left to right (or from top to bottom) is called **spatial organization**. It is up to you to give readers all the information they need. Remember to include information about sizes and shapes (a huge oval mirror), colors (a bright pink carpet), and textures (a lumpy sofa).

Study the picture some more and think about what you would see, hear, smell, feel, and taste if you were standing in the room. Now, write a description of the room in the picture. Give details in order from left to center to right.

_____

_____

_____

_____

Lesson 3 This Is A Room

Think of a room in your own home. It might be your bedroom or another room. Close your eyes and imagine it. What is on the left, center, and right? Make some notes about the room here. Remember to use sense words.

Now, write a paragraph in which you describe this room. Again, use spatial organization to present details from left to right to describe what you would see in the room.

_____

_____

_____

_____

_____

_____

_____

_____

_____

_____

Questions to Ask About a Descriptive Paragraph

Does the paragraph give details that clearly describe the place?
Does the paragraph present ideas in an order that makes sense, such as from left to right?
Does the paragraph use sense words so that readers can see, hear, smell, feel, and taste what is being described?
Is the first sentence of the paragraph indented?

Lesson 4 Imagine a Setting

You are writing a great story. Where does the action take place? Is it in a mad scientist's laboratory? In a desert? In a space-age classroom? Where the story happens is part of the setting.

First, write down as many ideas for story settings as you can think of. Even if an idea doesn't seem really interesting, list it here anyway. You might end up combining ideas.

Setting ideas: _____ _____ _____

_____ _____ _____

Now, think about when your great story will take place: in the past, in the present, or in the future. Time is also part of the setting. Imagine each place you listed above in the past, present, and future. Write your favorite idea below.

Place: _____

Time: _____

What is there to see? What sounds and smells are there? What textures and tastes?

Sights: _____

Sounds: _____

Smells: _____

Textures: _____

Tastes: _____

Review the details you have recorded. Can you really imagine the place?

Lesson 4 Imagine a Setting

Now, describe the setting of your story. Remember to organize your details in a way that makes sense. For example, if you are describing a room, you might go from left to right. If you are describing a tall rocket ship, you might go from bottom to top. If you are describing an outdoor setting, you might go from near to far. Think about which method makes most sense for your setting.

_____

_____

_____

_____

_____

_____

_____

_____

_____

_____

_____

On Your Own

Now that your setting is ready, write the story on a separate piece of paper. You may use the description of the setting as is, or you can write details from the description into your story as needed.

Lesson 5 Vary Sentence Structure

Mark wrote a description of his uncle's barn.

> In the barn, there are many things to see. In the hayloft, hay bales are piled high. On the wall, there are tools hanging all in a row. In the pen, sheep make soft little sounds. Through the stall windows, the horses beg for sugar.

Mark's paragraph is well organized, but it is not interesting. He started every one of his sentences with the same type of phrase that tells *where*. His description would be more interesting if he used sentences of different lengths and with different word order. Here is a revised version of Mark's paragraph. Notice that the words are almost exactly the same.

> There are many things to see in the barn. Hay bales are piled high in the hayloft. Tools hang on the wall. They are all in a row. Sheep make soft little sounds in their pen. The horses beg for sugar through the stall windows.

Write a description of this farm scene. In your paragraph, use a variety of short, medium, and long sentences. Do not begin all of your sentences the same way.

_____

_____

_____

_____

_____

_____

_____

Lesson 5 Vary Sentence Structure

Using short, medium, and long sentences in your writing helps it to be more interesting. Here are some other ways to make your sentences different and more interesting.

Begin with a word or phrase that tells *where*.	Over the barn roof, the sun rose.
Begin with a word or phrase that tells *when*.	In the morning, I like to be in the barn.
Begin with a word that tells *how*.	Slowly, I climbed up the wooden ladder.
Begin with the subject.	The barn is my favorite place to be.
Begin with action.	Pitching hay for the horses is hard work.

Write another description. It may be of the barn scene on page 92, or you may choose to describe something else. Keep in mind all of the ways to make your sentences different.

_____

_____

_____

_____

_____

_____

Lesson 6 The Writing Process: Descriptive Writing

Writers use descriptive writing in many ways. Descriptive writing can play a big part is some stories. It is also important in nonfiction. We are going to use your own experience as the base for a descriptive passage. You will describe observations you have made or events you have seen.

First, review the steps of the writing process.

> **Prewrite:** Choose a topic. Collect ideas. Make lists or charts. Organize ideas.
>
> **Draft:** Write ideas down on paper in sentences.
>
> **Revise:** Fix mistakes in draft. Add details. Change things around to make the writing better. Rewrite the sentences.
>
> **Proofread:** Check for final mistakes in spelling, capitalization, and punctuation.
>
> **Publish:** Make a final, error-free copy. Share with readers.

Prewrite

Your descriptive writing may take the form of an observation report, such as watching a plant grow and develop. Your descriptive writing may take the form of an eyewitness account, such as watching a storm from the safety of your home. Start by simply listing your first ideas about observations you have made or events you have seen.

_____   _____

_____   _____

_____   _____

Lesson 6 The Writing Process: Descriptive Writing

Choose one idea from page 94 that you think might work. In the space below, freewrite for two minutes, writing down absolutely everything you can think of about the idea.

Did your thoughts flow freely, or did you struggle to find things to write down? If you wrote easily, there's a good chance that the idea will work. If you had a hard time thinking of anything, choose another idea and freewrite about it on a separate sheet of paper. Continue until you find a topic idea about which your ideas flow easily.

Once you decide on a topic, you can collect details. Use this chart to record details. Use information from your freewriting, and write new ideas.

What I Saw	What I Heard	What I Smelled

What I Felt	What I Tasted

Lesson 6 The Writing Process: Descriptive Writing

So far, you have been choosing a topic, collecting ideas, and recording details. Now, it is time to put your ideas in order. Think about the event you will relate in your descriptive writing. Use the sequence chart on this page to list the events in order.

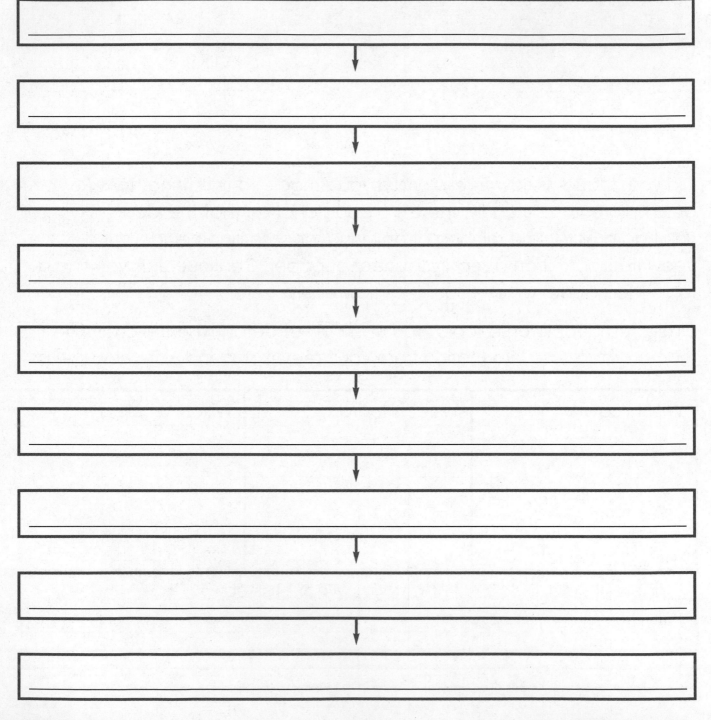

Lesson 6 The Writing Process: Descriptive Writing

Draft

Now, it is time to write a first draft of your descriptive writing. Write your draft on this page. Look back at your sequence chart on page 96 whenever you need to. As you write, don't worry about misspelling words or getting every word exactly right. Just get your main ideas down in sentences and in order.

_____

_____

_____

_____

_____

_____

_____

_____

_____

_____

_____

_____

Write an idea for a title here. It is okay if it changes later.

Title: _____

Lesson 6 The Writing Process: Descriptive Writing

Revise

You worked hard to put your ideas on paper. You must now imagine that someone else wrote it. You must read your own work as if you have never seen it before. This is a hard job. But if you look at the writing with "new eyes," you are more likely to spot mistakes or problems.

Answer the questions below about your draft. If you answer "no" to any of these questions, those are the areas that might need improvement. Feel free to make marks on your draft so you know what needs more work.

- Did you keep your audience in mind? Did you include details that will interest them and that they will understand?
- Did you make your first sentence especially interesting so that readers will want to continue reading?
- Did you tell events in order? Did you use time-order words to make it clear when events happened?
- Did you use spatial words to show where things are?
- Did you use sense words? To how many of your readers' senses did you appeal?
- Did you use sentences of different lengths and styles to keep your writing interesting?

Read your draft again and underline words that tell how something looked, sounded, smelled, felt, or tasted. Is there one in every sentence? Are there just a few? Look carefully to see where you could add descriptive words to make your description stronger. Here is how Kathy changed a sentence in her draft.

After the concert, the crowd was ~~loud~~. roaring

Lesson 6 The Writing Process: Descriptive Writing

Write the revision of your first draft below. As you revise, remember to make sure your order is clear and your description appeals to readers' senses.

_____

_____

_____

_____

_____

_____

_____

_____

_____

_____

_____

_____

_____

_____

_____

If you need to change your title, write the new title below.

Title: _____

Lesson 6 The Writing Process: Descriptive Writing

Proofread

It is best to proofread for just one kind of error at a time. First, read through your passage once for capital letters. Read it again for end punctuation. Then, read it again for spelling. Here is a checklist to help you as you proofread your revised descriptive writing.

_____ Each sentence begins with a capital letter.

_____ Each sentence ends with the correct punctuation (period, question mark, or exclamation point).

_____ Each sentence states a complete thought.

_____ All words are spelled correctly.

_____ Each paragraph begins with an indented sentence.

When proofreaders work, they use certain symbols. Using these symbols makes their job easier. They will make your job easier, too.

- <u>T</u>hree little lines under a letter mean that something should be capitalized. Write the capitalized letter above it.

- If there is a period missing, do this⊙

- Can you insert a question mark like this?

- Don't forget your exclamation points!

- Fix misspelled words like t͟h͟i͟s͟.

- Make this mark (¶) to show where to indent a paragraph.

Use these symbols as you proofread your descriptive writing. Remember to read your writing out loud. Sometimes it is easier to catch mistakes when reading out loud.

Lesson 6 The Writing Process: Descriptive Writing

Publish

Write a final copy of your personal narrative below. Write carefully and neatly so that there are no mistakes.

_____

_____

_____

_____

_____

_____

_____

_____

_____

_____

_____

_____

_____

_____

_____

_____

_____

Chapter 6
Lesson 1 A Story Line

A **story** tells about made-up people or animals. They are the **characters** in the story.

A story has a **setting** telling where and when the action takes place.

A story has a **plot**, or series of events, with a problem that needs to be solved.

An interesting **beginning**, a **middle**, and **end** make a story fun to read.

Describing words tell about the characters, setting, and events.

Read this story. Think about what happens at the beginning, in the middle, and at the end.

Max's Message

Today was Max's teacher's birthday, and Max woke up late. He scrambled around the house to get ready, brushing his teeth while pulling on his white socks. He grabbed a fresh apple from the kitchen on his way to the bus stop. He made it to the bus stop just as the bright yellow school bus was pulling up.

After Max hung up his red winter coat, he sat down at his desk in the middle of the room. Max then realized that he had forgotten Ms. Emery's birthday card at home. He hadn't put it in his backpack last night, and he had forgotten to grab it from the kitchen table on his way out. What was he going to do?

It was too cold outside to have recess, so Ms. Emery brought out the art supplies, and the students spent their recess drawing and writing. Max drew a huge birthday cake, with glowing candles and five layers. He wrote his name and took it up to Ms. Emery.

"Happy birthday, Ms. Emery," Max said.

Lesson 1 A Story Line

Answer these questions about "Max's Message." Look back at the story on page 102 if you need to.

Who are the characters in the story?

_____   _____

The action takes place in two settings. What are they?

_____   _____

What is the problem that Max has to solve?

_____

What happens at the beginning, in the middle, and at the end of the story?

Beginning	Middle	End

How does the writer describe the apple and the school bus? Find these and other describing words. List them here.

_____   _____

_____   _____

_____   _____

Lesson 2 Tell Me a Story

Do you like stories about dragons? Maybe you prefer stories with animals that talk. Or, maybe your favorite characters are from the planet Jupiter. Stories like these are called **fantasy**. Their characters could not be real or the events could not actually happen.

List some stories or books you have read that are fantasies:

_____ _____

_____ _____

What kind of fantasy would you like to write? Will you set it in a city in space or under the ocean? Maybe your main character has a special power of some sort. Let your imagination go and write down a couple of fantasy story ideas here.

Fantasy idea #1

Character(s): _____

Setting: _____

Plot: _____

_____

Fantasy idea #2

Character(s): _____

Setting: _____

Plot: _____

_____

Lesson 2 Tell Me a Story

Stories that include normal people who live on Earth are called **realistic**. Though their characters come from a writer's imagination, they could be real, and the events could actually happen.

List some stories or books you have read that are realistic:

_____   _____

_____   _____

What kind of realistic story would you like to write? Will it be about something funny that happens to an ordinary kid or a lost dog trying to find its way home? Realistic stories require just as much imagination as fantasies do. Jot down some realistic story ideas here.

Realistic story idea #1

Character(s): _____

Setting: _____

Plot: _____

_____

Realistic idea #2

Character(s): _____

Setting: _____

Plot: _____

_____

Lesson 3 Make Your Characters Speak

Dialogue is the conversation between characters in a story. When a writer uses dialogue in a story, the characters seem more real. Here is what dialogue looks like.

> "Has anyone seen Tippy?" Sharon asked. Her parents both shook their heads.
> "No, I haven't seen him, dear," said Dad.
> "Not since supper time," agreed Mom.
> Sharon swallowed. "I think he's lost," she squeaked, trying not to cry.

Take a closer look at a line of dialogue.

Quotation marks go before and after the speaker's exact words.

"No, I haven't seem him, dear," said Dad.

A **comma** separates the speaker's words from the tag line. It goes inside the ending quotation mark.

The **tag line** tells who is speaking.

Dialogue should sound like real people talking. An eight-year-old character should sound like a kid. A king should sound like a king. It wouldn't seem right to have a king say, "Hi, buddy. What's up?" would it? A king would probably say, "Hello, young man. How are you today?"

Write a line of dialogue for each character below. Make sure it sounds right based on the information about the character. Remember to use quotation marks, tag lines, and commas.

Mom, an important businesswoman: _____

_____

A young child who is lost in a store: _____

_____

Lesson 3 Make Your Characters Speak

Dialogue tells us more than what characters say. We learn about characters both by what they say and how they say it. We also learn about a character from what other characters say about him or her. Dialogue keeps readers interested and moves the story along.

Read the following lines of dialogue. Then, answer the questions.

> "Did you see a book lying on my desk, Mary?" asked Charles.
> "Why would I take your old book?" Mary challenged.
> "Because you would do anything to have something to read," Charles answered.
> Mary snorted, "Well, I can't help it if I don't have any money."
> Charles looked at Mary a long time. "Just give it back to me when you're done."

What do you know about Charles from these few lines of dialogue?

_____

_____

_____

What do you know about Mary? _____

_____

What do you know about the setting? _____

_____

What do you know about the plot? What do you think might happen next?

_____

_____

_____

NAME _____

Lesson 4 Make up a Simile

Sometimes, the goal of writing is to create a
picture for the reader. One way to create a
vivid picture is to use a **simile**. In a simile, two
things that are not alike are compared, using
the word *like* or *as*. The first sentence in the
paragraph below is a simile. It compares snow
to a blanket. What kind of picture does it create in your mind?

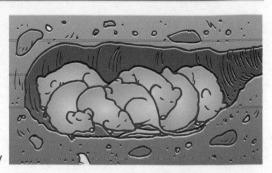

>   Snow lay on the field like a blanket. Underneath it, mice scurried in their grassy
> tunnels. They were happy and safe underneath the warm covering.

Here is another simile. What pictures does it create for you?

>   In their burrow, the mice snuggled together. They fit together like puzzle pieces,
> side to side and end to end.

In this simile, how mice snuggle together is compared to how puzzle pieces
fit together. Adding the simile in the second sentence creates a vivid
picture.

Some similes are very common. They usually involve comparing the color
of something to the color of something else.

>   Her hair was *as black as coal*.

>   The tree's yellow leaves glowed *like flames*.

Try some similes on your own. Complete each simile with at least one word
that creates a picture in your mind.

My face turned as red as _____

The old man's hair was as white as _____

The storm clouds rolled in like _____

Lesson 4 Make up a Simile

Similes do not always deal with color. They might relate to how something looks, sounds, feels, or tastes. Here are some more examples.

The little mouse looked *as soft as velvet*.

Her ears were *like little saucers* perched atop her head.

The snap of the trap was *like an explosion*. Mice scattered everywhere.

Remember, similes are all about creating images. Use your senses and your imagination and create some great images. Remember that you must use *like* or *as* in your comparison.

Write a simile in which you compare some detail about an animal to something else. Here is an example.

The frightened cat stopped; its tail stuck up like an antenna.

Write a simile about a sound.

_____

Write a simile about a texture or how something feels.

_____

Write a simile about how something looks.

_____

Write another simile about an object in the room around you.

_____

Lesson 5 Tell a Tall Tale

A **tall tale** is a special kind of story. In addition to made-up characters, it uses humor and exaggeration to tell its story. Exaggeration is when a writer stretches the truth and makes things larger, smaller, stronger, or different from how they really are. Here are some examples of exaggeration.

The wind blew so hard that the house tipped over.

My sister made such a fuss that they must have heard her in China.

Like a simile, exaggeration creates pictures for readers. With exaggeration, though, the picture is usually funny and often ridiculous.

Use exaggeration to complete these sentences.

Last winter it was so cold that _____

My turtle can run as fast as _____

He snored so loud, it sounded like _____

Jordan is so tall that _____

I felt so weak I couldn't even _____

It was so quiet you could hear _____

On Your Own

Exaggerations are fun to write and fun to draw. Complete this sentence.

Super Girl is so strong that she can _____

_____.

What picture does this bring to mind? Draw it on a separate sheet of paper. Then, write the sentence below the picture. Write more exaggerations and draw pictures. Make a book of exaggerations to share with your friends.

Lesson 5 Tell a Tall Tale

Now, think about writing a tall tale. Most tall tales involve a series of unusual events. The main character solves his or her problem with amazing cleverness or sometimes just incredibly good luck. Create a main character for your tall tale. Write some ideas here about your character. Remember to exaggerate how the character looks or acts.

Character's name: _____

How the character looks: _____

_____

What the character does or can do: _____

_____

Now, think about some unusual events. What kind of trouble does your character have? How does your character get out of trouble? List the main events of your tall tale below.

Character's problem

How character solves problem

How the story ends

Lesson 5 Tell a Tall Tale

Review the ideas about your character and his or her problems and
solutions. Now, write a first draft of your tall tale here. Remember to
introduce your character at the beginning, give your character a problem
to try to solve in the middle, and show how the problem is solved at the
end.

_____

_____

_____

_____

_____

_____

_____

_____

_____

_____

_____

_____

Questions to Ask About a Tall Tale

Does it have a beginning, middle, and an end?
**Does its character have a problem? Does the
character solve the problem?**
Does it use exaggeration? Is it funny?
Does the language create pictures for your readers?

Lesson 6 The Writing Process: Story

Writing a story can take you into a different world or help you express your ideas about your own world. First, review the steps of the writing process.

Prewrite: Choose a topic. Collect ideas. Make lists or charts. Organize ideas.

Draft: Write ideas down on paper in sentences.

Revise: Fix mistakes in draft. Add details. Change things around to make the writing better. Rewrite the sentences.

Proofread: Check for final mistakes in spelling, capitalization, and punctuation.

Publish: Make a final, error-free copy. Share with readers.

Prewrite

Stories can be completely different, but they all have certain features.

- A story tells about made-up **characters**—people, animals, or both.
- A story has a **setting** that tells where and when the action takes place.
- A story has a **plot** that includes a problem that needs to be solved.
- An interesting **beginning**, **middle**, and **end** make a story fun to read.
- **Describing words** tell about the characters, setting, and events.

Look at the story ideas you developed on pages 104 and 105. Choose one of those ideas and begin to explore it here.

_____

_____

_____

_____

Lesson 6 The Writing Process: Story

Now, work on the character of your story. Use this idea web to record details about how he or she looks, acts, speaks, and so on.

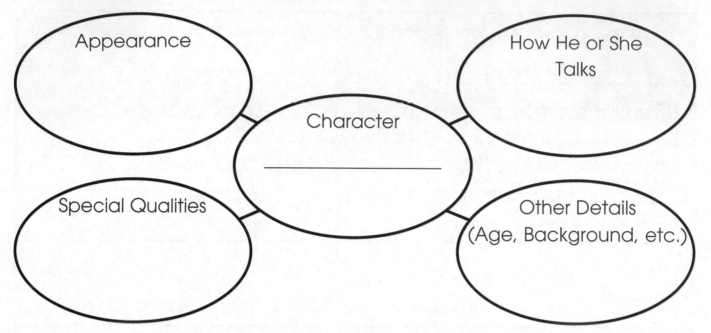

Answer these questions about your setting and plot.

What is the setting of your story? Consider these issues: place or location, season, time of day, weather conditions.

_____

_____

What is the character's problem?

_____

_____

What does the character do to try to solve the problem? Does it take more than one try?

_____

_____

Lesson 6 The Writing Process: Story

So far, you have chosen a topic and collected ideas. Now, it is time to put your ideas in order. Think about the story you are about to tell. Use the story map on this page to list the important parts of your story.

Character(s)
_____

Setting
_____

Problem
_____

Plot: Beginning
_____
_____
_____

Plot: Middle
_____
_____
_____

Plot: End
_____
_____
_____

Lesson 6 The Writing Process: Story

Draft

Write your story on this page, using your story map on page 115. As you write, don't worry about misspelled words or perfect punctuation. Just write your ideas down in sentences that are in order.

_____

_____

_____

_____

_____

_____

_____

_____

_____

_____

_____

_____

_____

Write an idea for a title here. You can change it later if you wish.

Title: _____

Lesson 6 The Writing Process: Story

Revise

As you begin to revise your own draft, try to pretend that you are reading the work for the very first time. This will help you find any mistakes.

Answer the questions below about your draft. If you answer "no" to any of these questions, those are the areas that might need improvement. Feel free to make marks on your draft, so you know what needs more work.

- Did you give details about an interesting character and a setting?
- Did you include a problem and a solution in your plot?
- Did you tell events in an order that made sense?
- Did you create pictures in your readers' minds with well-chosen words?
- Did you use dialogue to help readers learn about characters and to move the story forward?
- Did you enclose characters' words in quotation marks?
- Did you describe how things look, sound, smell, feel, and taste?
- Did you use sentences of different lengths and styles?

Kristi began to write a story. Here are some examples of punctuating dialogue. Notice how the tag lines, quotation marks, and commas are used.

"Where did you go for so long?" Ma called when she saw Pa.

Pa put down the sack he was carrying. It was about the size of a tractor. "Well, there weren't any potatoes in town," he answered.

"So, what did you do?" asked Ma, curiously.

Pa spoke proudly, "Well, I just dug some up along the way back home."

Ma was shocked. "You don't mean you dug up Mr. Spencer's potatoes!" she cried.

Lesson 6 The Writing Process: Story

Write the revision of your first draft here. As you revise, remember to make your characters say things that sound natural.

_____

_____

_____

_____

_____

_____

_____

_____

_____

_____

_____

_____

_____

_____

Are you still happy with your title? If not, write a new title below.

Title: _____

Lesson 6 The Writing Process: Story

Proofread

It is best to proofread for just one kind of error at a time. First, read through your story once for capital letters. Read it again for end punctuation. Then, read it again for spelling. Here is a checklist to help you as you proofread your revised story.

_____ Each sentence begins with a capital letter.

_____ Each sentence ends with the correct punctuation (period, question mark, or exclamation point).

_____ Dialogue is punctuated correctly.

_____ Each sentence states a complete thought.

_____ All words are spelled correctly. (If you're not sure, check a dictionary.)

When proofreaders work, they use certain symbols. Using these symbols makes their job easier. They will make your job easier, too.

- <u>T</u>hree little lines under a letter mean that something should be capitalized. Write the capitalized letter above it.

- Write in a missing end mark like this: ⊙ ? !

- Add a comma and quotation marks like this" he said.

- Fix misspelled ~~worlds~~ **words** like this.

Use these symbols as you proofread your story. Remember to read your writing out loud. Sometimes it is easier to catch mistakes when reading out loud.

Lesson 6 The Writing Process: Story

Publish

Write a final copy of your story below. Write carefully and neatly so that there are no mistakes. Then, think of ways to share your story.

_____

_____

_____

_____

_____

_____

_____

_____

_____

_____

_____

_____

_____

_____

Writer's Handbook

Writing Basics

Sentences are a writer's building blocks. To be a good writer, one must first be a good sentence writer. A sentence always begins with a capital letter.

>**He** walked around the block.

A sentence must always tell a complete thought. It has a subject and a predicate.

>Complete Sentence: He lives around the corner.
>Incomplete Sentence: The block where he lives.

A sentence always ends with an end mark. There are three kinds of end marks. A sentence that tells something ends with a period.

>He walked around the block**.**

A sentence that asks something ends with a question mark.

>Did he walk around the block**?**

A sentence that shows excitement or fear ends with an exclamation point.

>He ran all the way around the block**!**

Punctuation can be a writer's road map.

End marks on sentences show whether a sentence is a statement, a question, or an exclamation.

Commas help keep ideas clear.

>In a list or series: I saw sea stars, crabs, and seals at the beach.
>In a compound sentence: I wanted a closer look, but the crab crawled away.
>After an introductory phrase or clause: Later that day, a storm blew up.
>To separate a speech tag: I called to Mom, "It's really getting windy!"
>   "I hope it doesn't rain," she said.

Quotation marks show the exact words that a speaker says. Quotation marks enclose the speaker's words and the punctuation marks that go with the words.

>"Does it matter?" Neil remarked. "We're already wet."
>"I'd rather be wet from below than from above," said Dad.
>"Be careful!" Mom yelled. "Those waves are getting big!"

Writer's Handbook

The Writing Process

When writers write, they take certain steps. Those steps make up the writing process.

Step 1: Prewrite

First, writers choose a topic. Then, they collect and organize ideas or information. They might write their ideas in a list or make a chart and begin to put their ideas in some kind of order.

Mariko is going to write about her neighborhood. She put her ideas in a web.

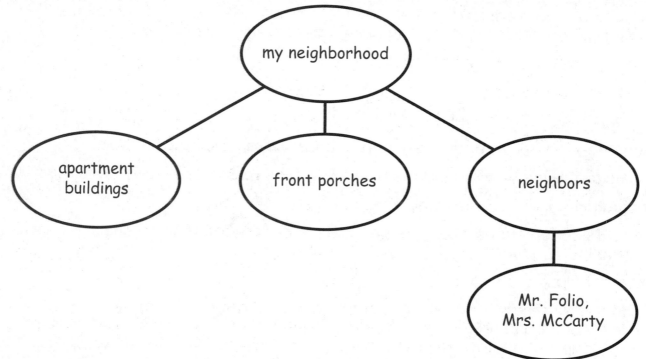

Step 2: Draft

Next, writers put their ideas on paper in a first draft. Writers know that there might be mistakes in this first draft. That's okay. Here is Mariko's first draft.

> Brick apartment houses are all around me. I live in tallest one. Across the street is the shortest. I like to think of the windows as eyes. and the front porches are the mouths People go in and out. Mr. Folio, my favorite neighbor, sits and sings songs. Mrs. McCarty pretends to shake a rug out the window but she is really listening to Mr. Folio.

Writer's Handbook

Step 3: Revise

Then, writers change or fix their first draft. They might decide to move ideas around, add information, or take out words or sentences that don't belong. Here are Mariko's changes.

> Brick apartment houses are all around me. I live in ᴬthe tallest one. ~~Across the street~~
> ~~is the shortest.~~ I like to think of the windows as eyes. and the front porches are the
> mouths People go in and out. Mr. Folio, my favorite neighbor, sits ᴬon his porch and sings ᴬItalian songs.
> ᴬIn the evening, Mrs. McCarty pretends to shake a rug out the window but she is really listening to
> Mr. Folio.

Step 4: Proofread

Writers usually write a new copy so their writing is neat. Then, they look again to make sure everything is correct. They look for mistakes in their sentences. Mariko found several more mistakes when she proofread her work.

> Brick apartment houses are all around me. I live in the tallest one. I like to think of
> the windows as eyes, and ~~the~~ front porches ᴬas ~~are the~~ mouths. People go in and out. Mr.
> Folio, my favorite neighbor, sits on his porch and sings Italian songs. In the evening,
> Mrs. McCarty pretends to shake a rug out the window, but she is really listening to
> Mr. Folio.

Step 5: Publish

Finally, writers make a final copy that has no mistakes. They might choose to add pictures and create a book. Then, they are ready to publish their writing. They might choose to read their writing out loud or have a friend read it.

Writer's Handbook

Personal Narrative

In a personal narrative, a writer writes about something she has done or seen. It might tell about something funny, sad, or unusual. A personal narrative can be about anything, as long as the writer is telling about one of his or her own experiences. Here is the final version of Mariko's paragraph about her neighborhood.

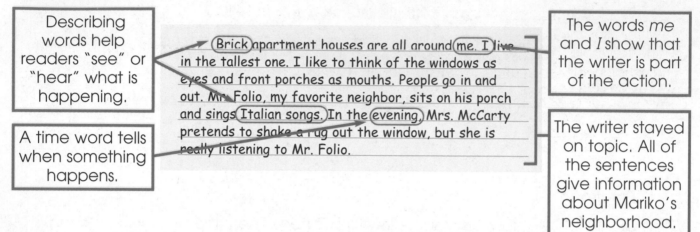

Describing words help readers "see" or "hear" what is happening.		The words *me* and *I* show that the writer is part of the action.

Brick apartment houses are all around me. I live in the tallest one. I like to think of the windows as eyes and front porches as mouths. People go in and out. Mr. Folio, my favorite neighbor, sits on his porch and sings Italian songs. In the evening, Mrs. McCarty pretends to shake a rug out the window, but she is really listening to Mr. Folio.

A time word tells when something happens.

The writer stayed on topic. All of the sentences give information about Mariko's neighborhood.

Stories

Writers write about made-up things. They might write about people or animals. The story might seem real, or it might seem fantastic, or unreal. Here is a story that Mariko wrote. It has both human and animal characters in it. The animals speak, so Mariko's story is not realistic.

The story has a beginning, a middle, and an end.

The first paragraph establishes the setting.

In the Neighborhood

It is nearly sunrise, and the neighborhood is waking up. Windows glow where the early birds prepare breakfast. Bacon sizzles in the Hooper kitchen, and the smell draws a hungry crowd.

In the corner, eight furry paws scramble through the crack between the wall and the baseboard. They pause at the corner of the wastebasket, then scamper to the refrigerator. Blue fuzzy slippers come quickly forward and stamp on the floor. "Go away, you critters!" The critters huddle deeper in the darkness. Four black eyes watch for crumbs to fall. Two long tails twitch with excitement.

Mrs. Hooper's slippers scuff across the floor. "It's ready!" she calls upstairs. In a moment, Mr. Hooper's heavy work boots thump down the stairs. *Scuff-thump*, *Scuff-thump*, the people go into the other room.

"Now, it's our turn," smiles Velvet.

Her brother Flannel nods and shrugs. "It's a dirty job, but someone has to do it." And he and his sister go to work, clearing the floor of crumbs.

Sensory words help readers visualize what is happening.

Time and order words keep ideas in order.

The story includes dialogue, or conversation among characters.

This story is written in third-person point of view. So, words such as *he*, *she*, *her*, *his*, and *they* refer to the characters.

Writer's Handbook

Descriptive Writing

When writers describe, they might tell about an object, a place, or an event. They use sensory words so that readers can see, hear, smell, feel, or taste whatever is being described. In this example of descriptive writing, Mariko compared her old bedroom with her new bedroom.

> The writer uses the whole-to-whole comparison method. She describes one whole room in the first paragraph, and the other room in the second paragraph.

    My bedroom in our old apartment was green. It was a nice grassy green, and it always made me think of a forest. My bed was in the left corner, between the two windows. The wall straight ahead was almost all shelves, where I kept my turtle collection, my books, and all my other stuff. My yellow beanbag chair and the closet were on the right side of the room.
    My new bedroom is blue. I like to think of it as sky blue. On the left side of the room is one big window. I put my beanbag chair right beside the window. Straight ahead is my bed. On the right is a built-in bookshelf and the closet door.

> Sensory details help readers visualize the scene.

> The writer organizes details from side to side. She first tells what is on the left, then straight ahead, then on the right.

Informational Writing

When writers write to inform, they present information about a topic. Informational writing is nonfiction. It is not made up; it contains facts.

Mariko interviewed her neighbor, Mr. Folio. Then, she wrote about what she learned. Here is one of her paragraphs.

> Mariko states her main idea in a topic sentence. It is the first sentence of the paragraph.

> Transition words connect ideas.

    My neighbor, Mr. Folio, has lived in the same apartment building all his life. His parents and his grandparents lived there, too. In fact, his grandparents were the first people to move into the building in 1921. He remembers his grandmother telling about how new and shiny the doorknobs and the stair railings were. Mr. Folio's grandparents lived on the top floor because his grandfather liked the view. Later, his parents lived on the fourth floor because that was what was available at the time. Now, Mr. Folio lives on the first floor. He says he likes to see what is going on in the neighborhood.

> These sentences contain details that support the main idea.

Writer's Handbook

Explanatory (or How-to) Writing

Writers explain how to do things. They might write about how to play a game, create an art project, or follow a recipe. Mariko has written instructions for a marble game that she plays with her sister.

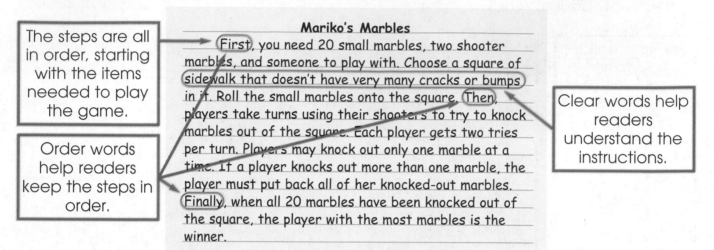

The steps are all in order, starting with the items needed to play the game.

Order words help readers keep the steps in order.

Mariko's Marbles

First, you need 20 small marbles, two shooter marbles, and someone to play with. Choose a square of sidewalk that doesn't have very many cracks or bumps in it. Roll the small marbles onto the square. Then, players take turns using their shooters to try to knock marbles out of the square. Each player gets two tries per turn. Players may knock out only one marble at a time. If a player knocks out more than one marble, the player must put back all of her knocked-out marbles. Finally, when all 20 marbles have been knocked out of the square, the player with the most marbles is the winner.

Clear words help readers understand the instructions.

Persuasive Writing

In persuasive writing, writers try to make readers think, feel, or act in a certain way. Persuasive writing shows up in newspaper and magazine articles, letters to the editor, business letters, and in advertisements, of course. Mariko's mom has written a letter to the editor of the local newspaper.

The writer begins by stating some opinions.

The writer uses an emotional appeal to persuade readers to agree with her.

Dear Editor:

    I used to be proud of my neighborhood. The streets used to look nice, and people cared about keeping them that way. Now, however, the sidewalks on 41st Street are terribly cracked and broken, and the city has no plans to fix them. In some places, it is not even safe to walk. The older people in the neighborhood have to walk in the street to get to the grocery store. Can't the city repair the sidewalks? It would feel good to be proud and safe in my neighborhood again.

                         F. Torunaga

The writer states some facts to lend support to her opinions.

The writer includes a specific request for action.

Writer's Handbook

Friendly Letters

Writers write friendly letters to people they know. They might share news or ideas or request information. A friendly letter has four parts: the date, the greeting, the body, and the closing, which includes the signature. Here is a letter Mariko wrote to her grandfather.

Each word in the greeting begins with a capital letter.

There is always a comma after the person's name.

The date is in the upper, right corner.

The body of the letter gives information.

Only the first word of the closing begins with a capital letter. There is always a comma after the closing.

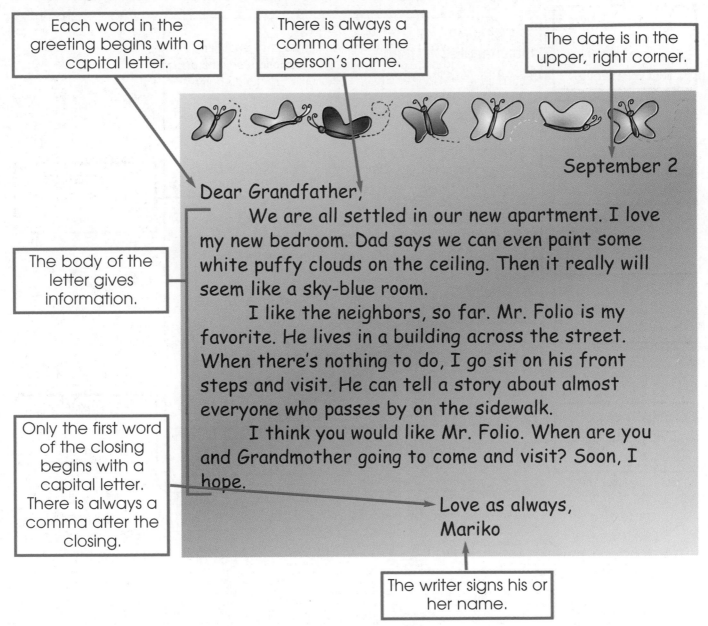

September 2

Dear Grandfather,

　　We are all settled in our new apartment. I love my new bedroom. Dad says we can even paint some white puffy clouds on the ceiling. Then it really will seem like a sky-blue room.

　　I like the neighbors, so far. Mr. Folio is my favorite. He lives in a building across the street. When there's nothing to do, I go sit on his front steps and visit. He can tell a story about almost everyone who passes by on the sidewalk.

　　I think you would like Mr. Folio. When are you and Grandmother going to come and visit? Soon, I hope.

Love as always,
Mariko

The writer signs his or her name.

Writer's Handbook

Business Letters

Writers write business letters to people or organizations with whom they are not familiar. Business letters usually involve a complaint or a request for information. Mariko needs information for a school report. She wrote a business letter to request information.

The heading includes the sender's address and the date.

764 41st Street
Indianapolis, IN 46208
October 5, 2007

The inside address is the name and address of the recipient.

Monroe County Historical Society
202 E. 6th Street
Bloomington, IN 47402

Dear Monroe County Historical Society:

The greeting is followed by a colon.

My class is studying state history this year. Each of us has chosen a county to study. I chose Monroe County because my grandparents live there.

On your Web site, I saw that you have a free pamphlet titled "Monroe County: Through the Years." Please send me one copy of that brochure. I have included an envelope with postage.

Thank you for your help with my report.

Sincerely,

Mariko Torunaga

Mariko Torunaga

The text of the letter is the body.

The sender always includes a signature.

The closing is followed by a comma.

Answer Key

Chapter 1

Lesson 1

Page 5
Animals and plants live in the desert.

Page 6
Answers will vary.

Lesson 2

Page 7
Circled titles:
Alex's Bad Day
Building for Tomorrow
School Days Return

Page 8
Titles will vary.

Lesson 3

Page 9
Circled titles:
A New Home for Turtle
Rainy Day Drawing

Page 10
Titles will vary.

Lesson 4

Page 11
Circled main ideas:
The games we play have been around
    for many years.
I got ready for school early.

Page 12
Main ideas will vary.

Lesson 5

Page 13
Circled errors:
cage My
week. best

Page 14
Paragraphs will vary.

Page 15
Paragraphs will vary.

Lesson 6

Page 16
Crossed-out sentences:
When I was little, I took dancing lessons.
Next week, I hope to have some flowers
    to plant.

Page 17
Crossed-out sentence:
I have a dress with lots of bright colors.
Paragraphs will vary.

Answer Key

Chapter 2

Lesson 1

Page 19
Order of steps, as shown:
Step 2: Draft
Step 4: Proofread
Step 1: Prewrite
Step 5: Publish
Step 3: Revise

Lesson 2

Page 20
Lists will vary.

Page 21
Lists will vary.

Lesson 3

Page 22
Lists will vary.

Page 23
Lists will vary.

Lesson 4

Page 25
Idea webs will vary.

Lesson 5

Page 26
Charts will vary.

Page 27
Charts will vary.

Lesson 6

Page 28
Time words and phrases will vary.
Sentences will vary.

Page 29
Circled transition words:
Then, Later

Underlined time words:
half an hour, the day, late
Sentences will vary.

Lesson 7

Page 30
Sentences and paragraphs will vary.

Page 31
Descriptions will vary.

Page 32
Descriptions will vary.

Lesson 8

Page 33
News articles will vary.

Page 34
Responses will vary.

Lesson 9

Page 35
Diagrams will vary.

Page 36
Diagrams and sentences will vary.

Lesson 10

Page 37
Stone Mountain is shorter than Rock
   Mountain.
Sal is sadder than Hal.
Hal is happier than Sal.

Page 38
Sentences will vary.
Tim is the shortest player.

Page 39
Kite 3 has the longest tail.
Kite 2 has the shortest tail.
Responses will vary.

Answer Key

Chapter 3

Lesson 1

Page 40
Journal entries will vary.

Page 41
Entries will vary.

Lesson 2

Page 42
Responses will vary.

Page 43
Paragraphs will vary.

Lesson 3

Page 44
Responses will vary.

Page 45

> July 6
>
> Dear Jennifer,
>   Thank you for your letter, dear. Fluffy is much better, now.
>   I remember seeing Fluffy with that napkin. I went to the kitchen right after that. I had the giggles, too!
>   Love,
>   Grandma

Lesson 4

Page 46
date
greeting
body
closing
Notes will vary.

Page 47
Letters will vary.

Lesson 5

Page 48
Responses will vary.

Page 49
Letters will vary.

Lesson 6

Page 51
Responses will vary.

Lesson 7

Page 52
Responses will vary.

Page 53
Responses will vary.

Page 54
Sequence charts will vary

Page 55
First drafts will vary.

Page 57
Revisions will vary.

page 59
Personal narratives will vary.

Answer Key

Chapter 4

Lesson 1

Page 60
sentence: <u>The storm</u> (came suddenly.)
fragment (missing a subject)
fragment (missing a predicate)

Page 61
run-on (corrected to: I heard a crash. It was up in the kitchen.)
run-on (corrected to: Mom went upstairs, but I stayed in the basement. OR Mom went upstairs. I stayed in the basement.)
sentence
run-on (corrected to: It was the cat, and he had knocked over a plant. OR It was the cat. He had knocked over a plant.)

Lesson 2

Page 63
<u>Tyler</u>
X <u>Popcorn</u>
X <u>Mrs. Kraft</u>
X <u>The mess</u>

Lesson 3

Page 64
Lists will vary.

Page 65
Lists will vary.

Lesson 4

Page 66
O
F
O

Page 67
Opinions and facts will vary.

Lesson 5

Page 68

Students should circle sentences 1 and 3.

Page 69
Lists will vary.

Lesson 6

Page 70
Instructions will vary.

Page 71
Instructions will vary.

Lesson 7

Page 72
(First,) go (down) this hallway. When you get to the (end,) turn (left.) Walk (past) the main office. (Then), the nurse's office is the (second) door on the (right.)

Page 73
Directions will vary.

Lesson 8

Page 74
Questions will vary.

Page 75
Questions will vary.

Lesson 9

Page 76
Possible topics will vary.

Page 77
Responses will vary.

Page 78
Chart entries will vary.

Page 79
First drafts will vary.

Page 81
Revised news stories will vary.

Page 83
Final news stories will vary.

Answer Key

Chapter 5

Lesson 1
Page 84
Listed items will vary.

Page 85
Paragraphs will vary.

Lesson 2
Page 86
Responses will vary.

Page 87
Riddles will vary.

Lesson 3
Page 88
Descriptions will vary.

Page 89
Paragraphs will vary.

Lesson 4
Page 90
Responses will vary.

Page 91
Descriptions will vary.

Lesson 5
Page 92
Descriptions will vary.

Page 93
Descriptions will vary.

Lesson 6
Page 94
Responses will vary.

Page 95
Responses will vary.

Page 96
Charts will vary.

Page 97
First drafts will vary.

Page 99
Revisions will vary.

Page 101
Final descriptions will vary.

Answer Key

Chapter 6

Lesson 1

Page 103
Max, Ms. Emery
Max's house, a classroom
He forgot Ms. Emery's birthday card at home.
Beginning: Max slept in and was almost late.
Middle: Max noticed that he forgot Ms. Emery's birthday card at home.
End: Max draws a birthday card for her.
"fresh apple," "bright yellow school bus"; Other descriptive words will vary.

Lesson 2

Page 104
Responses will vary.

Page 105
Responses will vary.

Lesson 3

Page 106
Dialogue will vary.

Page 107
Possible answers:
Charles may be older than Mary. Charles "has money."
Mary likes to read. She doesn't "have any money."
The setting is in a room with a desk.
The plot might have to do with Mary taking things that don't belong to her. It might have something to do with finding a way for Mary to get things to read. It might have to do with how Charles helps Mary.

Lesson 4

Page 108
Similes will vary.

Page 109
Similes will vary.

Lesson 5

Page 110
Sentences will vary.

Page 111
Responses will vary.

Page 112
Tall Tales will vary.

Lesson 6

Page 113
Story ideas will vary.

Page 114
Chart entries and responses will vary.

Page 115
Story map entries will vary.

Page 116
First drafts will vary.

Page 118
Revisions will vary.

Page 120
Final stories will vary.

Notes